ATILLA SHRUGGED

ATILLA SHRUGGED

AYN RAND,
WORMWOOD STAR OF THE APOCALYPSE

A Mash-up
By Fyodor Dostoyevsky
And Sally Brent

CHIRINGAPRESS
SEGUIN, TEXAS

Chiringa Press
© Copyright 2011 Michael Godeck
All Rights Reserved

ISBN 978-1-61012-011-1

eBook: ISBN 978-1-61012-012-8
Audio edition: ISBN 978-1-61012-013-5
Red Letter edition, with the words of Ayn in Red:
    ISBN 978-1-61012-014-2

Typeset in Ideal Sans
 (not to be confused with Sans Ideals)

mgodeck@chiringapress.com
www.speedofdark.com

The rich grind the poor into abjectness and then complain that they are abject.

They goad them to famine, then hang them if they steal a sheep.

—Percy Bysshe Shelley

αψίνθιον

And the third angel sounded, and there fell a great star from heaven, burning as it were a lamp, and it fell upon the third part of the rivers, and upon the fountains of waters;

And the name of the star is called Wormwood: and the third part of the waters became wormwood; and many men died of the waters, because they were made bitter.

—The Apocalypse of John

"I swear by my life and my love of it that I will never live for the sake of another man, nor ask another man to live for mine!"

—The Galtian Oath

Table of Contents

Preface 11
Acknowledgements 13
Foreword 17
Cast of Characters 19
Character Sketches 21
A Summary of the Action 25

Atilla Shrugged

Act I — The Destroyer
Scene I — First Eddie 33
Scene II — Interview with the Destroyer 35
Scene III — Delirium in Atlantis 47
Scene IV — Interview with the Destroyer 51
Scene V — Delirium in Atlantis 53
Scene VI — Interview with the Destroyer 59
Scene VII — Delirium in Atlantis 61
Scene VIII — Interview with the Destroyer 65

Act II — The Police Inspector
Scene I — Second Eddie 75
Scene II — Interview with the Police Inspector 79

Act III — The Wormwood Star
Scene I - Third Eddie 91
Scene II — Of Railways 95
Scene III — John Henry 109

Musical Scores 111
Illustrations 119

Songs

A is A 47
Workin' on the Railroad Line 61
A Little Talk with Dagny 74
O It's Goin' to be a Mighty Day 94
John Henry 105

Preface

As I watched Alan Greenspan make his chastened confession of having uncovered a flaw in his theory of self-interest as it applies to the fulfillment of fiduciary responsibility, I wondered if perhaps it would have been better had he foregone his illustrious career and, from his days as a tender foundling of the Randian clique, to have put that clever mind of his on strike, stoically withholding the bounty of his demiurgic intellect.

I imagined Lloyd Blankfein as a Galtian *destroyer*, calling on those great men who carry the weight of the world on their shoulders: the leviathans of Goldmen Sachs, Lazard Frères and JP Morgan, inducing them to forsake their benevolent yet misguided efforts for the betterment of their brothers.

Lloyd would bring them around to the very conclusions that they themselves had already secretly reached, but were reluctant to admit, even to themselves. With the benefit of the destroyer's guidance, they would come to see the futility of continuing to serve the common herd of whining, lying and chiseling humanity demanding that they had a *right* to the return of capital so fairly lost on the field of battle in the holy crusade for accelerated returns at compound interest.

Lloyd met his critics head-on with an uncomplicated declaration: "I am doing God's work!"

With the Titanic pride of a man-god, legitimately ordering his life as he pleases, gathering together the chosen few to Galt's Gulch, to wait out the inevitable dissipation of our pathetic wrath and the final collapse of a decadent civilization. Then the creators would return together in triumph to show those of us who had somehow survived without them, how it's done.

Forward

Had we thought things through, we might have ceded Lloyd and his friends the prison island of Zanzibar for their purpose. For some reason, we went in for their shell-game of credit default swaps instead.

The curious legacy of Ayn Rand, champion of the irascible self-made man, is that the greatest looters in the history of Man carry her portrait around in their wallets.

Alan Greenspan qualified his remarks by saying: "I really didn't get it until very late in 2005." In all fairness to Ayn, all the way back when *"I like Ike"* still had currency, she seemed to have an inkling of where we were headed, writing:

> "He was seeing the enormity of the smallness of the enemy who was destroying the world. He felt as if, after a journey of years through a landscape of devastation, past the ruins of great factories, the wrecks of powerful engines, the bodies of invincible men, he had come upon the despoiler, expecting to find a giant—and had found a rat eager to scurry for cover at the first sound of a human step. If this is what has beaten us, he thought, the guilt is ours."
>
> —*Atlas Shrugged*
> Chapter IV — *The Sanction of the Victim*

Acknowledgements

On first approaching Fyodor about this project, I had scant hope that he would be inclined to attend to what amounted to little more than my wild fantasy. To begin with, he was unfamiliar with Ayn Rand's works. This should come as no surprise, since it has been some time since he had been a regular at those soireés where one might have occasion to witness a Randian Ideal brandished in defense of the swipes and jabs of some leprous humanitarian, the likes of whom can be counted on to impose herself on better company, no matter how carefully the guest list is managed. Nonetheless, he was considerate, and took the time to hear me out. He had, as he related, time on his hands.

At first he was incredulous, but then, as he read Ayn for himself, a sort of appreciation seemed to grow, and at times he became downright excited; agitated even. Through the months of our collaboration, we met in Stockholm and sometimes in Dallas, and we talked into the night, often ending in a quarrel. He would break off and swear that he was through with me and my 'damnedable project', (as he called it), but I suspected his affection was actually growing. Each time he returned and began by urging me to desist and insisting that his participation should remain anonymous in any case. Gradually, it became evident that he was hooked.

The turning point came one night after we went to see the movie, *Atlas Shrugged, Part I*. It was an upscale place, where they serve dinner and drinks in the theater. As the final credits scrolled, he sat in silence, nursing his whiskey.

I took his silence as reverence matching mine. At last he exclaimed, softly, as if to no one: "She is the wormwood."

Acknowledgments

More than a bit surprised, but not wanting to reveal that I had no idea what he was talking about, I repeated, putting on an informed, inquisitive aspect: *"Wormwood?"*

"The Third Angel ... it is her." The ice cubes tinkled as he swirled his liquor.

I had always revered Ayn, but I had never thought of her as among the Angels. *"Which* angel?" I inquired, as if it were a dispute over the proper angelic selection.

He had gone off on a jag like this before, and I knew there was no stopping him. He stood. His voice let loose like thunder: *"And when he had opened the seventh seal, there was silence in heaven about the space of half an hour!"* I'm sure you know the rest.

The remaining customers made for the door and the girl cleaning up the dinner trays stopped to call for backup on her walkie-talkie. Fyodor bellowed on, from the fire cast down from heaven to the catastrophe of the Wormwood Star. A security guard stumbled down the aisle with one hand on his Taser, but owning that he was a Seventh-Day Adventist, he ended up rather as a backup for Fyodor. With authority clearly on his side, Fyodor ordered another round.

The security guard disputed, insisting that the Wormwood Star was Atilla, leader of the Huns, and this just fanned Fyodor's little grass-fire into the forest.

"Yes, yes!" he exclaimed. "The Huns left us very put out, but the Wormwood Star ... No! You cannot go so far!"

The Adventist produced the Wormwood Wikipedia page on his phone and began citing sources in defense of the Atilla theory. Fyodor would have none of it. The situation grew tense.

The clean-up girl returned with the drinks and the manager in tow, clearly intent on dousing the conflagration. The manager sized up the situation and broke in, interrupting Fyodor mid sentence, (something I'd never succeeded in doing).

"Chernobyl! It is Chernobyl, the Wormwood Star!" he burst in. With this, the clean-up girl threw in the towel. One fist to his breast, his right arm fully extended, he proclaimed *"a great star from heaven, burning as it were a lamp, and it fell upon the third part of the rivers, and upon the fountains of waters;"* Doubling down on the dramatic, he continued: *"And the name of the star is called Wormwood: and the third part of the waters became wormwood; and many men died of the waters, because they were made bitter."*

He finished and for a moment there was only the sound of clinking ice cubes. Fyodor sipped, as if nothing had happened.

The manager answered this pregnant moment with a single word for emphasis: *"Chernobyl"*. Clearly he felt he had overcome all opposition. The security guard was frenetically poking his smart-phone, searching for sources that might restore his Atilla theory, while the clean-up girl looked on hopefully from a distance.

Fyodor began speaking slowly, directly, emphatically, admonishing the manager: "You imagine the waters were a fountain or stream?" There was an uncomfortable silence. The manager shuffled his feet as Fyodor pressed his point: "A mighty unstoppable river, perhaps?"

More silence. I knew Fyodor well enough by now to see that the dam was crumbling; that the torrent was about to break. The security guard and manager stood before the impending danger as deer in a spotlight. The clean up girl, already at a distance, took a step back, instinctively taking shelter behind a door frame.

"When Moses struck the rock, was it suddenly a gurgling stream that appeared?" The manager smiled weakly, suspecting that it might be a trick question, while the Seventh Dayer glanced nervously toward the exit.

"Or was it the very Word of God that issued forth?" He prodded their reticence, interjecting: "Eh?"

Fyodor then burned off Psalm 114, and preceded to feed the flames, throwing on Ezekiel 36:25, Hebrews 10:22, Isaiah 55:1, Jeremiah 2:13 and finally, towering over his little congregation, belted out John 14:4. I had no idea. The manager and the Adventist looked like little scorched shrubs.

Fyodor sat down in perfect tranquility and took up his drink. He sipped. Then he said softly, as if to children: "No. The water is the Word; the one who made the thoughts of men bitter, the Wormwood."

I was indignant. "You can't be speaking of the producers! The very creators! Without them there would be no events!"

Can you believe he called me naïve? That's just how it was.

Sally Brent
Austin, Texas
September 11, 2011

Foreword

When *The Fountainhead* became fashionable among the architectural set, Ayn Rand was not pleased. When the readers of the New York Times were advised that it was an interesting novel about architecture, she was offended and outraged; evidently the reviewer identified with Ellsworth Toohey. Whatever his motives, certainly we can conclude that the central theme of *The Fountainhead* is something decidedly more than the raising of roofs.

I am sympathetic with Ms. Rand on this account, because I still burn with indignation when I remember how *The Overcoat* became a sort of cult classic among tailors. I was expecting that I would finally get some recognition and respect from the critics; instead, all I got was some overstuffed personage calling on me about an honorary membership in the Moscow tailor's guild. Needless to say, I threw him out and spoke with no one for a week, I was so angry. I can only imagine how Ayn felt, so you may appreciate the extent to which I sympathize with the million ways in which her work has been misunderstood.

An ordinary writer will anguish over the blankness of the paper before them, scouring his brain for some notion that might impress itself upon the mind of the reader as so entirely uncommon as to be astonishing, whereas Ayn possessed a genius which surpassed that great ocean of mediocrity.

The thing that first impressed me about Ayn was her mastery of ideas that a less audacious author might have rejected as thread-worn; too shabby to provide protection against the cruel winter winds, which, (according to St. Petersburg custom), blowing from all four directions at once, leave one scampering for the shelter of the nearest doorway, and so, perhaps, to fall into bad company. The mediocre author will naturally shy away from such risks, and cleave to more reliably popular themes.

Introduction

In contrast, Ayn started with little more than an old cloak made on an Aristotelian loom from the golden days of Feudalism, which, having been worn by the aristocracy all the way through the Enlightenment, the Industrial Age and on into our own Century of the Common Man, was as threadbare as the old overcoat of Akaky Akakievich.

This is the genius of Rand: that she was able to weave a renewed fabric from these seemingly spent scraps, so magnificent, so heroic, that it has become the foundation of an untrodden faith that seeks no lower object than to turn back Abraham and his Prophets, the Talmud and the New Testament, all in a throw.

Speaking as a writer who has spent many an afternoon, my chin planted in my palms, gazing into the lamp light of eternity, I can only express a sort of awesome admiration.

Nikolai Gogol
Sorochyntsi, Ukraine

Cast of Characters

ATILLA SHRUGGED

Sally Brent [4]
Fyodor Dostoyevsky

From whence ...	
The Brothers Karamazov [1]	The Fountainhead [4]
Crime and Punishment [2]	Atlas Shrugged [5]
The Idiot [3]	Ideal [6]
The Apocalypse of John [9]	

Eddie Willers [5] as himself
Eddie Willers as Ivan Karamazov[1]
Eddie Willers as Razumihin [2]
Eddie Willers as Nikolai Ardalyonovitch Ivolgin [3] (Kolya)
Bertram Scudder [5] as Gavril Ardalyonovich Ivolgin [3] (Gayna)
Mr. Thompson [5] as General Ivolgin [3]
Wesley Mouch [5] as Keller [3]
Johnnie Dawes [6] as Hippolyte [3]
Nat Taggart [5] as Rodion Romanovitch Raskolnikov [2]
Ayn Rand as the Third Angel of the Seventh Seal [9]
Policy Inspector Porfiry Petrovitch [2]
Prince Lev Nikolayevich Myshkin [3]
Lebedev [3]
Some Angels [9]
Satan, the Destroyer [9]

Special Guest Appearances:
  Francisco d'Anconia [5]
  Ragnar Danneskjöld [5]
  John Galt, the destroyer [5]

Character Sketches

Ayn Rand is best characterized by Fyodor, who offered: "Take the soul of an enlightened Russian atheist and mix it with the soul of the prophet Jonah, who sulked for three days and nights in the belly of the whale." You can take it from there.

Eddie Willers (*Atlas Shrugged*) interprets several roles from Dostoyevsky: the mercurial Ivan Karamazov in Act I, Raskolnikov's guileless friend Razumihin in Act II, and the smart, sensitive Kolya in Act III. He also plays his own doggedly loyal self in the John Galt monologues, which open each act.

Atlas Shrugged, Part I the movie casts Eddie Willers along the lines of a yuppie house-negro, wholesomely good, self-sacrificing and fatally loyal to his boss-lady, Dagny Taggart, yet falling short on that essential virtue which might get him an invitation to Galt's Gulch, its membership plan being *invitation only*.

Nathaniel 'Nat' Taggart (*Atlas Shrugged*) is the honored founder of Taggart Transcontinental Railroad, who is essential if sketchy backstory to the novel. He is the archetypal heroic man who triumphs in his own lifetime. The key to understanding this *exceptional man* is the legend of his having (allegedly) murdered a man, a Senator no less, who stood in the way of the construction of his rail line. The justification offered is strikingly similar to that of Raskolnikov (*Crime and Punishment*), who murdered the old pawn broker lady, because, (so it seemed to him at the time) she was an obstacle blocking the fulfillment of his destiny.

Prince Myshkin (*The Idiot*), is a fair-haired, blue-eyed epileptic in his late twenties who is innocent, naïve, impractical, compassionate, and immensely kind; to wit, the type of person Ayn despised.

Character Sketches

LEBEDEV (*The Idiot*), Prince Myshkin's landlord, is a bit of a wildcard: a widower; a drunkard with pretensions to become a lawyer. He is easily given over to telling stories of dubious veracity; renown for his interpretation of the *Apocalypse of John*.

POLICE INSPECTOR PORFIRY PETROVITCH (*Crime and Punishment*), is in his mid fifties, his hair cut short with a large round head. He has a soft, rather snub-nosed face with a sickly pallor. He is stout even to corpulence. Although his father is a government official, his steady professional rise is due to a habit of careful diligence and a practical, logical approach which has, over time, resolved some otherwise intractable quandaries.

WESLEY MOUCH (*Atlas Shrugged*) is a glad-handing, back-stabbing bureaucratic climber; the proverbial second-hander. Mouch interprets Keller (*The Idiot*) who is noble, whereas Mouch is a cad who will avoid any confrontation. Keller, on the other hand, will stand as a second in a duel. Still, both are essentially enforcers for more powerful players.

JONNIE DAWES (*Ideal*) interprets Fyodor's high-strung Hippolyte. (*The Idiot*). Both characters are rather live-wires fixated on the idea of winning the esteem of others through the unusually extreme personal sacrifice of a bullet through the head. Ayn allows that Jonnie succeeds whereas Fyodor spares Hippolyte.

BERTRAM SCUDDER (*Atlas Shrugged*) is a despicable lefty journalist who is not very inquisitive. He lives by the unexamined axiom that eating and drinking are the guiding principles of a man's life. He interprets Fyodor's Radomski (*The Idiot*), a bothersome clerk.

FRANCISCO D'ANCONIA, **RAGNAR DANNESKJÖLD**, and **JOHN GALT** (*Atlas Shrugged*), founding partners of Galt's Gulch: *The New Jerusalem*. High up on the mountain we find the few whose names are written in Galt's book of life, *where there shall be no more pain, for the former things have passed away*; while dogs, sorcerers and second-handers remain outside to suffer a second death. Ayn's heros have long since escaped from the pages of her novel to fulfill their Nietzschean destiny through the lives of impressionable readers. As Raskolnikov noted, '*young people are particularly apt to fall into that snare*'. The original trio make a guest appearance in *Atilla Shrugged* to proudly affirm the Galtian Oath.

Character Sketches

SATAN, THE DESTROYER, is forever cast as the scapegoat. Whatever character sketch we might propose, you will probably think us much the fool, for you're apt to say we know him not at all; perhaps you are already much better acquainted. In any event, our Fallen Angel, like John Galt, feels himself at odds with the world as we find it. The difference is that while the Galtian destroyer is intent on *stopping the motor of the world*, the original Destroyer has admitted a more ambiguous ambition, (according to Fyodor, anyway) saying: "*...I would give away all this super stellar life, all the ranks and honours, simply to be transformed into the soul of a merchant's wife weighing eighteen stone and set candles at God's shrine.*" So possibly the Devil is a more complicated cipher than you had imagined, after all.

"And godlike Ganymede, most beautiful of men; Galt beheld him and caught him up to heaven, so beautiful was he..."

A Summary of the Action

Atilla Shrugged does not seek to establish a parallel universe to *Atlas Shrugged*, but rather draws on the creative inspiration of Dostoyevsky, who contributed the majority of the prose. We invite you to consider the extent to which Fyodor anticipated Ayn, and perhaps even *intended* to preempt her line of reasoning. Our purpose is to clear some space to let Fyodor stand in on the question, according to what we insist was his intention.

You can think of our whole proposition as an heroic version of *The Nutcracker Suite*, with Eddie Willers as Clara. Like Clara, Eddie falls asleep after a long day at the office and dreams the muddled truth of his conflicted world. If it helps, you might think of Prince Myshkin as Dosselmeyer, (although you'll have to make some allowances).

Eddie's monologues with a mysterious companion are a central structural device of *Atlas Shrugged*. These late night encounters between Eddie and a lowly railroad worker in the underground cafeteria of the Taggart Transcontinental headquarters in New York City provide essential clues to where the story is going. Like our conversations with God, the other guy's side of the dialog is left pretty much to our imagination and, at the outset, we know nothing of this shadowy figure. Deeper into the novel, the stranger seems more like Eddie's confessor, and we begin to suspect that this tenebrous visitor is more important than his humble station suggests. As it turns out, the mysterious man is none other than John Galt, the destroyer.

Eddie Willers' conversations with John Galt from *Atlas Shrugged* are adapted to *Atilla Shrugged* as the opening scene to each act. An Eddie Willers monologue serves as introduction to his delirious conversation with the Destroyer (Act I — adapted from *The Brothers Karamazov*, where the scene with Ivan takes place on the eve of his brother Demitri's trial for the murder of their father, Fyodor Karamazov). In *Atilla*, this scene leads to Eddie's dream sequence of Ayn in the afterlife and only then, as the Devil says, does our story begin.

A Summary of the Action

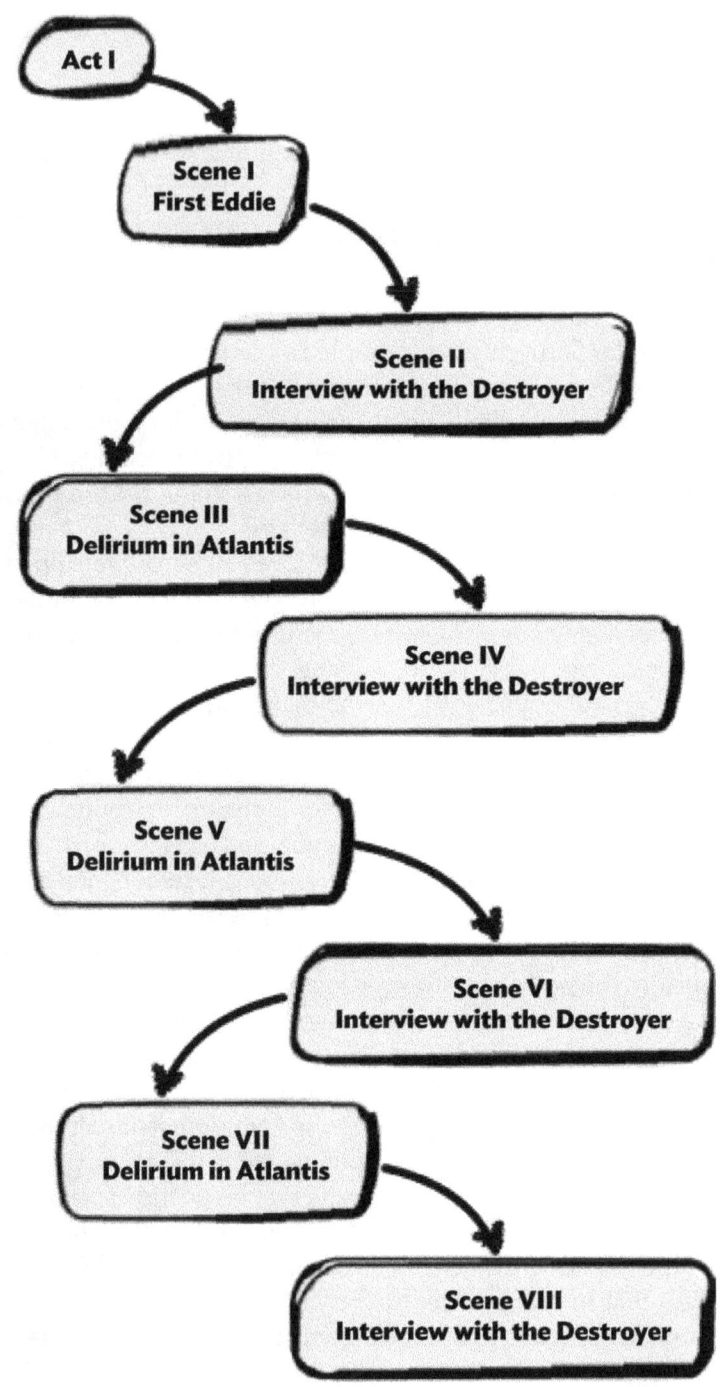

A Summary of the Action

Once in Paradise, Prince Myshkin applies the parable of the onion, (adapted from *The Brothers Karamazov)*, obtaining a provisional entry into Paradise for Ayn, the gate-crasher. The good Prince becomes her guide and leads her to an encounter with her mythical grandfather, Nathaniel Taggart, (Act II) who they find in the midst of an interview with the Police Inspector, (adapted from *Crime and Punishment*, wherein Porfiry Petrovich engages Raskolnikov in a discussion on a theory of crime and the *extraordinary* man. The scene takes place as Raskolnikov undertakes to dispel suspicion that it might be he, the murderer of the old pawn broker lady).

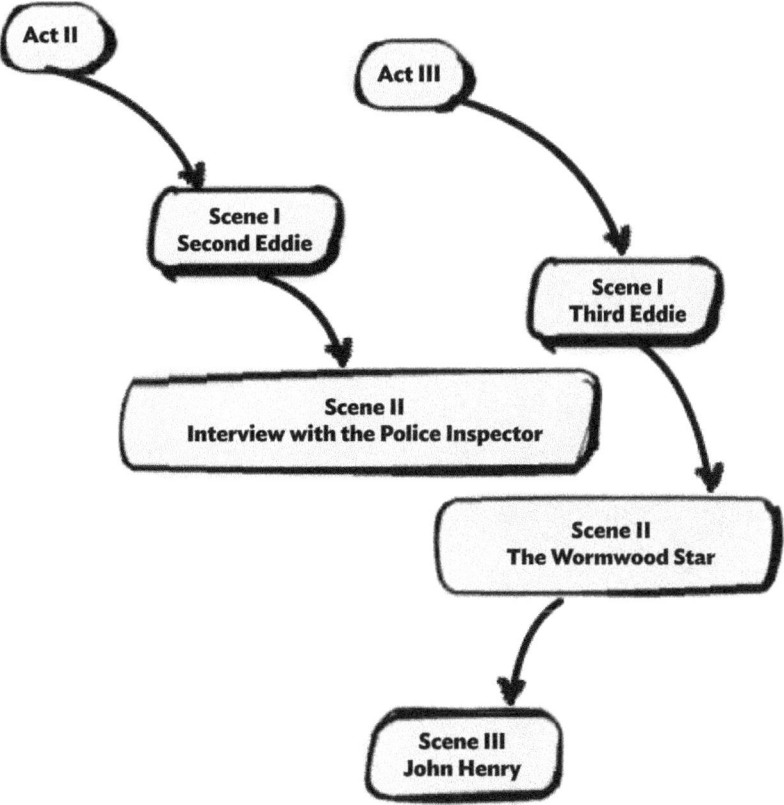

Finally, Ayn is reunited with her *Ideal Men*: Francisco d'Anconia, Ragnar Danneskjöld and John Galt (Act III) at a party at Prince Myshkin's Villa (adapted from *The Idiot*) outside the gates of Paradise, where Lebedev is goaded into defending his thesis of the Wormwood Star of the Apocalypse.

Atilla Shrugged

Act I
The Destroyer

"You'll kill me? No, excuse me, I will speak."

Scene I — First Eddie
"May God bless him wherever he is…"
"Atlas Shrugged"
Part I Chapter 3

Time: Late at night…

Place: In the Taggart Rail Terminal underground cafeteria.

Cast: Eddie Willers

Summary: Eddie Willers carries on an intense, one-sided conversation with a figure in the shadows.

ψ

Eddie is in a conversation with an unseen stranger, we cannot hear the responses…

Eddie Willers: "…That's what people are whispering…"

pauses to listen…

Eddie Willers, *answering*: "…The newspapers haven't printed a word about it."

listens…

Eddie Willers, *sarcastically*: "The boys in Washington say that it's only a rumor spread by panic-mongers."

listens briefly…

Eddie Willers, *uncertainly*: "I don't know whether the story is true." (*more definitely*) "I think it is." (*with conviction*) "I hope it is…"

Eddie Willers, *continues reflectively*: "You know, when I was fifteen years old, I used to wonder how any man could come to be a criminal, I couldn't understand what would make it possible. Now — I'm glad that Ragnar Danneskjöld blew up those towers. May God bless him and never let them find him, whatever and where ever he is."

pauses to listen…

Eddie Willers: "Yes. That's what I've come to feel. Well, how much do they think people can take?"

pauses briefly…

Eddie Willers: "It's not so bad for me in the daytime, because I can keep busy and not think, but it gets me at night. I can't sleep any more, I lie awake for hours …"

Transition to Eddie Willers apartment…

Scene II — Interview with the Destroyer
"I am Satan, and deem nothing human alien to me..."
"The Brothers Karamazov"
Part IV Book XI Chapter 9

Time: Late one night...

Place: Eddie Willers' living room.

Cast: Eddie Willers and the Devil.

Summary: Eddie Willers is disturbed after the events of the day, tense with uncertainty over what is to come; falls asleep on the sofa. When he wakes, the Devil is seated opposite him, waiting patiently. Eddie suspects the Devil might be himself; conversation ensues.

ψ

Eddie Willers, alone in his apartment; nervously pacing. He lies down on the sofa and falls asleep. When he wakes, he finds an unexpected visitor sitting opposite him, who looks much like himself, although apparently a Devil.

The countenance of the unexpected visitor is not so much good-natured, as accommodating and ready to assume any amiable expression as occasion might arise.

Eddie is angrily silent and will not begin the conversation. The visitor waits and sits exactly like a poor relation who has come down from his room to keep his host company at tea, and is discreetly silent, seeing that his host is frowning and preoccupied. But he is ready for any affable conversation as soon as his host should begin it. All at once his face expresses a sudden solicitude...

Devil: "I say, excuse me, I only mention it to remind you. You went to find the railway schedule, but you came away without finding out anything about it, you probably forgot..."

Eddie Willers, *with gloomy uneasiness*: "Ah, yes. Yes, I'd forgotten... but it doesn't matter now, never mind, till tomorrow."

Eddie Willers, *muttering to himself, addressing his visitor*: "...and you, I should have remembered that myself in a minute, for that was just what was tormenting me! Why do you interfere, as if I should believe that you prompted me, and that I didn't remember it of myself?"

Devil, *smiling amicably*: "Don't believe it then, what's the good of believing against your will? Besides, proofs are no help to believing, especially material proofs. Thomas believed, not because he saw Christ risen, but because he wanted to believe, before he saw. Look at the spiritualists, for instance.... I am very fond of them... only fancy, they imagine that they are serving the cause of religion, because the devils show them their horns from the other world. That, they say, is a material proof, so to speak, of the existence of another world. The other world and material proofs, what next! And if you come to that, does proving there's a Devil prove that there's a God? I want to join an idealist society, I'll lead the opposition in it, I'll say I am a realist, but not a materialist, *he he!*"

Eddie Willers: *suddenly getting up from the table*: "Listen, I seem to be delirious... I am delirious, in fact, talk any nonsense you like, I don't care! You won't drive me to fury, as you did last time. But I feel somehow ashamed... I want to walk about the room.... I sometimes don't see you and don't even hear your voice as I did last time, but I always guess what you are prating, for it's I, myself, speaking, not you. Only I don't know whether I was dreaming last time or whether I really saw you. I'll wet a towel and put it on my head and perhaps you'll vanish into air."

> *Eddie goes to the corner, takes a towel, and does as he said, and with a wet towel on his head begins walking up and down the room.*

Devil: "I am so glad you treat me so familiarly!"

Eddie Willers: "Fool!" (*laughs*) "Do you suppose I should stand on ceremony with you? I am in good spirits now, though I've a pain in my forehead… only please don't talk philosophy, as you did last time. If you can't take yourself off, talk of something amusing. Talk gossip, you are a poor relation, you ought to talk gossip. What a nightmare to have! But I am not afraid of you. I'll get the better of you. I won't be taken to a mad-house!"

Devil: "*C'est charmant*, poor relation. Yes, I am in my natural shape. For what am I on earth but a poor relation? By the way, I am listening to you and am rather surprised to find you are actually beginning to take me for something real, not simply your fancy, as you persisted in declaring last time…"

Eddie Willers, *starting with a bit of fury*: "Never for one minute have I taken you for reality! You are a lie! You are my illness! You are a phantom! It's only that I don't know how to destroy you and I see I must suffer for a time. You are my hallucination. You are the incarnation of myself, but only of one side of me… of my thoughts and feelings, but only the nastiest and stupidest of them. From that point of view you might be of interest to me, if only I had time to waste on you…"

Devil: "Excuse me, excuse me, I'll catch you. When you flew out at James under the lamp-post this evening and shouted to him, 'You learnt it from him! How do you know that he visits me?' You were thinking of me then. So for one brief moment you did believe that I really exist." *laughs blandly*.

Eddie Willers: "Yes, that was a moment of weakness… but I couldn't believe in you. I don't know whether I was asleep or awake last time. Perhaps I was only dreaming then and didn't see you really at all…"

Devil: "And why were you so surly with James just now? He is a dear; I've treated him badly over Dagny."

Eddie Willers: "Don't talk of Dagny! How dare you, you flunky!" *Laughs again*.

Devil: "You scold me, but you laugh — that's a good sign. But you are ever so much more polite than you were last time and I know why: that great resolution of yours…"

Eddie Willers, *savagely*: "Don't speak of my resolution!"

Devil: "I understand, I understand, *c'est noble, c'est charmant*, you are going to defend the railroad and to sacrifice yourself… *C'est chevaleresque*."

Eddie Willers: "Hold your tongue, I'll kick you!"

Devil: "I shan't be altogether sorry, for then my object will be attained. If you kick me, you must believe in my reality, for people don't kick ghosts. Joking apart, it doesn't matter to me, scold if you like, though it's better to be a trifle more polite, even to me. 'Fool, flunky!' What words!"

Eddie Willers: "Scolding you, I scold myself!" (*laughs*) "You are myself, myself, only with a different face. You just say what I am thinking… and are incapable of saying anything new!"

Devil, *with delicacy and dignity*: "If I am like you in my way of thinking, it's all to my credit."

Eddie Willers, *through clenched teeth*: "You choose out only my worst thoughts, and what's more, the stupid ones. You are stupid and vulgar. You are awfully stupid. No, I can't put up with you! What am I to do, what am I to do?"

Devil: "My dear friend, above all things I want to behave like a gentleman and to be recognized as such."

Devil: *continues in a deprecating and simple-hearted pride, typical of a poor relation*: "I am poor, but… I won't say very honest, but… it's an axiom generally accepted in society that I am a fallen angel. I certainly can't conceive how I can ever have been an angel. If I ever was, it must have been so long ago that there's no harm in forgetting it. Now I only prize the reputation of being a gentlemanly person and live as I can, trying to make myself agreeable. I love men genuinely, yet I've been greatly calumniated! Here when I stay with you from time to time, my life gains a kind of reality and that's what I like most of all. You see, like you, I suffer from the fantastic and so I love the realism of earth. Here, with you, everything is circumscribed, here all is formulated and geometrical, while we have nothing but indeterminate equations! I wander about here dreaming. I like dreaming. Besides, on earth, I become superstitious. Please don't laugh, that's just what I like, to become superstitious. I adopt all your habits here: I've grown fond of going to the public baths, would you believe it? And I go and steam myself with merchants and priests. What I dream of is becoming incarnate once for all and irrevocably in the form of some merchant's wife weighing eighteen stone, and of believing all she believes. My ideal is to go to church and offer a candle in simple-hearted faith, upon my word it is. Then there would be an end to my sufferings. I like being doctored too; in the spring there was an outbreak of smallpox and I went and was vaccinated in a foundling hospital — if only you knew how I enjoyed myself that day. I subscribed ten roubles in the cause of the poor!... But you are not listening. Do you know, you are not at all well this evening? I know you went yesterday to that doctor... Well, what about your health? What did the doctor say?"

Eddie Willers, *snaps out*: "Fool!"

Devil: "But you are clever, anyway. You are scolding again? I didn't ask out of sympathy. You needn't answer. Now rheumatism has come in again..."

Eddie Willers: "Fool!"

Devil: "You keep saying the same thing; but I had such an attack of rheumatism last year that I remember it to this day."

Eddie Willers: "The Devil have rheumatism!"

Devil: "Why not, if I sometimes put on fleshly form? I put on fleshly form and I take the consequences. *Satan sum et nihil humanum a me alienum puto.*" *(I am Satan, and deem nothing human alien to me).*

Eddie Willers: "What, what, Satan *sum et nihil humanum*... that's not bad for the Devil!"

Devil: "I am glad I've pleased you at last."

Eddie Willers, *suddenly, seeming struck, stops*: "But you didn't get that from me. That never entered my head, that's strange."

Devil: "*C'est du nouveau, n'est-ce pas?*" *(It's new, isn't it?)* "This time I'll act honestly and explain to you. Listen, in dreams and especially in nightmares, from indigestion or anything, a man sees sometimes such artistic visions, such complex and real actuality, such events, even a whole world of events, woven into such a plot, with such unexpected details from the most exalted matters to the last button on a cuff, as I swear Leo Tolstoy has never invented. Yet such dreams are sometimes seen not by writers, but by the most ordinary people, officials, journalists, priests.... The subject is a complete enigma. A statesman confessed to me, indeed, that all his best ideas came to him when he was asleep. Well, that's how it is now, though I am your hallucination, yet just as in a nightmare, I say original things which had not entered your head before. So I don't repeat your ideas, yet I am only your nightmare, nothing more."

Eddie Willers: "You are lying, your aim is to convince me you exist apart and are not my nightmare, and now you are asserting you are a dream."

Devil: "My dear fellow, I've adopted a special method today, I'll explain it to you afterwards. Stay, where did I break off? Oh, yes! I caught cold then, only not here but yonder."

Eddie Willers, *almost in despair*: "Where is yonder? Tell me, will you be here long. Can't you go away?"

> *Eddie stops walking to and fro, sits down on the sofa, leans his elbows on the table again and holds his head tight in both hands. He pules the wet towel off and flings it away in vexation, evidently of no use.*

Devil, *with a carelessly easy, though perfectly polite, air*: "Your nerves are out of order. You are angry with me even for being able to catch cold, though it happened in a most natural way. I was hurrying then to a diplomatic soirée at the house of a lady of high rank in Petersburg, who was aiming at influence in the Ministry. Well, in an evening suit, white tie, gloves, though I was God knows where and had to fly through space to reach your earth.... Of course, it took only an instant, but you know a ray of light from the sun takes full eight minutes, and fancy in an evening suit and open waistcoat. Spirits don't freeze, but when one's in fleshly form, well... in brief, I didn't think, and set off, and you know in those ethereal spaces, in the water that is above the firmament, there's such a frost... at least one can't call it frost, you fancy, 150 degrees below zero! You know the game the village girls play — they invite the unwary to lick an axe in thirty degrees of frost, the tongue instantly freezes to it and the dupe tears the skin off, so it bleeds. But that's only in 30 degrees, in 150 degrees I imagine it would be enough to put your finger on the axe and that would be the end of it... if only there could be an axe there."

Eddie Willers, *interrupting, carelessly and disdainfully*: "And can there be an axe there?"

Eddie is exerting himself to the utmost not to believe in the delusion and not to sink into complete insanity.

Devil, *in surprise*: "An axe?"

Eddie, *suddenly, with a savage and insistent obstinacy*: "Yes, what would become of an axe there?"

Devil: "What would become of an axe in space? *Quelle idée!* If it were to fall to any distance, it would begin, I think, flying round the earth without knowing why, like a satellite. The astronomers would calculate the rising and the setting of the axe; Gatzuk would put it in his calendar, that's all."

Eddie Willers, *peevishly*: "You are stupid, awfully stupid, fib more cleverly or I won't listen. You want to get the better of me by realism, to convince me that you exist, but I don't want to believe you exist! I won't believe it!"

DEVIL: "But I am not fibbing, it's all the truth; the truth is unhappily hardly ever amusing. I see you persist in expecting something big of me, and perhaps something fine. That's a great pity, for I only give what I can..."

EDDIE WILLERS: "Don't talk philosophy, you ass!"

DEVIL: "Philosophy, indeed, when all my right side is numb and I am moaning and groaning. I've tried all the medical faculty: they can diagnose beautifully, they have the whole of your disease at their finger-tips, but they've no idea how to cure you. There was an enthusiastic little student here, *'You may die,'* said he, *'but you'll know perfectly what disease you are dying of!'* And then what a way they have of sending people to specialists! *'We only diagnose,'* they say, *'but go to such-and-such a specialist, he'll cure you.'* The old doctor who used to cure all sorts of diseases has completely disappeared, I assure you, now there are only specialists and they all advertise in the newspapers. If anything is wrong with your nose, they send you to Paris: there, they say, is a European specialist who cures noses. If you go to Paris, he'll look at your nose; *'I can only cure your right nostril',* he'll tell you, *'for I don't cure the left nostril, that's not my specialty, but go to Vienna, there there's a specialist who will cure your left nostril'.* What are you to do? I fell back on popular remedies, a German doctor advised me to rub myself with honey and salt in the bath-house. Solely to get an extra bath I went, smeared myself all over and it did me no good at all. In despair I wrote to Count Mattei in Milan. He sent me a book and some drops, bless him, and, only fancy, Hoff's malt extract cured me! I bought it by accident, drank a bottle and a half of it, and I was ready to dance, it took it away completely. I made up my mind to write to the papers to thank him, I was prompted by a feeling of gratitude, and only fancy, it led to no end of a bother: not a single paper would take my letter. *'It would be very reactionary,'* they said, *'none will believe it. Le diable n'existe pas."* (*The Devil does not exist*). *"You'd better remain anonymous.'* they advised me. What use is a letter of thanks if it's anonymous? I laughed with the men at the newspaper office; *'It's reactionary to believe in God in our days,'* I said, *'but I am the Devil,* *so I may be believed in.' 'We quite understand that,' they said. 'Who doesn't believe in the Devil? Yet it won't do, it might injure our reputation. As a joke, if you like.'* But I thought as a joke it wouldn't be very witty. So it wasn't printed. And do you know, I have felt sore about it to this day. My best feelings, gratitude, for instance, are literally denied me simply from my social position."

EDDIE WILLERS, *snarling malignantly:* "Philosophical reflections again?"

DEVIL: "God preserve me from it, but one can't help complaining sometimes. I am a slandered man. You upbraid me every moment with being stupid. One can see you are young. My dear fellow, intelligence isn't the only thing! I have naturally a kind and merry heart. I also write vaudevilles of all sorts. You seem to take me for Hlestakov grown old, but my fate is a far more serious one. Before time was, by some decree which I could never make out, I was predestined *to deny* and yet I am genuinely good-hearted and not at all inclined to negation. *'No, you must go and deny, without denial there's no criticism and what would a journal be without a column of criticism?'* Without criticism it would be nothing but one *hosannah*. But nothing but hosannah is not enough for life, the hosannah must be tried in the crucible of doubt and so on, in the same style. But I don't meddle in that, I didn't create it, I am not answerable for it. Well, they've chosen their scapegoat, they've made me write the column of criticism and so life was made possible. We understand that comedy; I, for instance, simply ask for annihilation. 'No, live', I am told, 'for there'd be nothing without you. If everything in the universe were sensible, nothing would happen. There would be no events without you, and there must be events.' So against the grain I serve to produce events and do what's irrational because I am commanded to. For all their indisputable intelligence, men take this farce as something serious, and that is their tragedy. They suffer, of course... but then they live, they live a real life, not a fantastic one, for suffering is life. Without suffering what would be the pleasure of it? It would be transformed into an endless church service; it would be holy, but tedious. But what about me? I suffer, but still, I don't live. I am x in an indeterminate equation. I am a sort of phantom in life who has lost all beginning and end, and who has even forgotten his own name. You are laughing — no, you are not laughing, you are angry again. You are forever angry, all you care about is intelligence, but I repeat again that I would give away all this super stellar life, all the ranks and honors, simply to be transformed into the soul of a merchant's wife weighing eighteen stone and set candles at God's shrine."

EDDIE WILLERS, *with a smile of hatred*: "Then even you don't believe in God?"

DEVIL: "What can I say? — that is, if you are in earnest..."

EDDIE WILLERS, *with the same savage intensity*: "Is there a God or not?"

DEVIL: "Ah, then you are in earnest! My dear fellow, upon my word I don't know. There! I've said it now!"

EDDIE WILLERS: "You don't know, but you see God? No, you are not someone apart, you are myself, you are I and nothing more! You are rubbish, you are my fancy!"

DEVIL: "Well, if you like, I have the same philosophy as you, that would be true. *Je pense, donc je suis.*" *(I think, therefore I am)* "I know that for a fact; all the rest, all these worlds, God and even Satan — all that is not proved, to my mind. Does all that exist of itself, or is it only an emanation of myself, a logical development of my ego which alone has existed forever: but I make haste to stop, for I believe you will be jumping up to beat me directly."

EDDIE WILLERS, *miserably*: "You'd better tell me some anecdote!"

DEVIL: "There is an anecdote precisely on our subject, or rather a legend, not an anecdote. You reproach me with unbelief; you see, you say, yet you don't believe. But, my dear fellow, I am not the only one like that. We are all in a muddle over there now and all through your science. Once there used to be atoms, five senses, four elements, and then everything hung together somehow. There were atoms in the ancient world even, but since we've learned that you've discovered the chemical molecule and protoplasm and the Devil knows what, we had to lower our crest. There's a regular muddle, and, above all, superstition, scandal; there's as much scandal among us as among you, you know; a little more in fact, and spying, indeed, for we have our secret police department where private information is received. Well, this wild legend belongs to our middle ages — not yours, but ours — and no one believes it even among us, except the old ladies of eighteen stone, not your old ladies I mean, but ours. We've everything you have, I am revealing one of our secrets out of friendship for you; though it's forbidden. This legend is about Paradise. There was, they say, here on earth a thinker and philosopher. She rejected everything, *laws, conscience, faith*, and, above all, the future life. She died; she expected to go straight to darkness and death but she found a future life before her. She was astounded and indignant..."

Transition to Paradise...

Scene III — Delirium in Atlantis
"A is A"

"ATLAS SHRUGGED" PART III – CHAPTER 1
"THE BROTHERS KARAMAZOV" PART III BOOK VIII CHAPTER 8

Time: Eternity...

Place: Paradise.

Cast: Ayn Rand,
   The Angel Gabriel,
   A Host of Angels.

Summary: Ayn Rand crash-lands her plane in a mountain valley somewhere in heaven. Faced with the unexpected prospect of an afterlife, she is indignant.

ψ

The sound of an solitary single engine airplane. One can hear the plane begin to circle in a canyon. The sound becomes distressed: something is wrong. The sound is of a plane going into a death spiral, and then a terrible crash.

Silence.

Ayn is lying injured. A man leans over her.

AYN, *as if in a dream*: "We never had to take any of it seriously, did we?"

GABRIEL: "No, we never had to."

Ayn, realizing that the man is a total stranger, tries to draw away, but winces in pain.

GABRIEL: "Don't move, Miss Rand. You're hurt"

AYN, *impersonal and hard:* "You know me?"

GABRIEL: "I've known you many years."

AYN: "Have I known you?"

GABRIEL: "Yes, I think so."

AYN: "What is your name?"

GABRIEL: "I am Gabriel, guardian of this place..."

> Ayn looks at him not moving. More Angels step in from the shadows.

GABRIEL: "Why are you frightened?"

AYN: "Because I believe it." (*pauses*) "What is this place?"

GABRIEL: "Some people refer to it as *Paradise,* some say it is *Atlantis,* but I think of it as the *Taggart Terminal.*"

AYN, *dazed:* "...Taggart Terminal?"

GABRIEL, *proudly:* "...Last big stop in the sky..."

AYN, *in sudden fury* "This is outrageous! This is against my principles!"

> All look to this strange new arrival.

AN ANGEL, *perplexed:* "Outrageous?"

ANOTHER ANGEL, *doubtfully, inquiringly:* "Principles?"

AYN, *resolute:* "By what right did you make it sound like I — I! — gave my sanction for this!"

AN ANGEL: "...Sanction?"

ANOTHER ANGEL: "...Right?"

AYN, *less certain:* "...Step aside you hatred-eaten mystics, posing as friends of humanity!"

An Angel: "You would prefer not to exist?"

Ayn: "Existence exists!"

An Angel: "It seems you are faced with a contradiction. Perhaps you should first check your principles..."

Ayn, *cutting him off*: "Death is the standard of your existence!"

Another Angel, *helpfully*: "...perhaps the Angels aren't?"

> *An angel choir forms and begins singing:*
>
> **A is A**
> *—to the tune of "God is God": (Key of C)*
>
> *A is an A, A don't never change!*
> *A is an A, An' it always will be A!*
>
> *A made the sun to shine by day,*
> *A made the sun to show the way.*
> *A made the stars to show their light,*
> *A made the moon to shine by night, sayin'*
>
> *A is an A, A don't never change!*
> *A is an A, An' it always will be A*
>
> *The earth A's footstool an' heav'n A's thrown,*
> *The whole creation all its own,*
> *A's love and power will prevail*
> *A's promises will never fail, sayin'*
>
> *A is an A, A don't never change!*
> *A is an A, An' He'll always will be A*

Ayn, *defiant*: "Damnation is the start of your morality, destruction its purpose, means and end!"

An Angel, *conciliatory*: "Don't let's quarrel..."

Ayn, *defiant*: "I don't work with collectives. I don't consult, I don't cooperate, I don't collaborate."

An Angel, *perplexed:* "Collectives?"

Another Angel, *doubtfully, inquiringly:* "Collaborate?"

Another Angel: "But why is she even here, at the gate?"

Ayn, *defiant:* "Yes, why? No other sanction than my existence is necessary!"

Transition to Eddie Willers' apartment...

Scene IV — Interview with the Destroyer
"Well, is she lying there now?"
"The Brothers Karamazov" Part IV Book XI Chapter 9

Time: Late one night...

Place: Eddie Willers' living room.

Cast: Eddie Willers and the Devil.

Summary: Eddie Willers and the Destroyer discuss the nature of crime and divine punishment.

ψ

Eddie's interview with the Devil resumes...

Devil, *continues:* "...She was astounded and indignant. '*This is against my principles!*' she said. And she was punished for that... that is, you must excuse me, I am just repeating what I heard myself, it's only a legend... she was sentenced to walk a quadrillion kilometers in the dark (we've adopted the metric system, you know) and when she has finished that quadrillion, the gates of heaven would be opened to her and she'll be forgiven—"

Eddie Willers, *with strange eagerness:* "And what tortures have you in the other world besides the quadrillion kilometers?"

Devil: "What tortures? Ah, don't ask. In the old days we had all sorts, but now they have taken chiefly to moral punishments — *the stings of conscience* and all that nonsense. We got that, too, from you, from the softening of your manners. And who's the better for it? Only those who have got no conscience, for how can they be tortured by conscience when they have none? But decent people who have conscience and a sense of honor suffer for it. Reforms, when the ground has not been prepared for them, especially if they are institutions copied from abroad, do nothing but mischief! The ancient fire was better. Well, this woman, who was condemned to the quadrillion kilometers, stood still, looked round and lay down across the road. *'I won't go, I refuse on principle!'* Take the soul of an enlightened Russian atheist and mix it with the soul of the prophet Jonah, who sulked for three days and nights in the belly of the whale, and you get the character of that thinker."

EDDIE WILLERS: "What did she lie on there?"

THE DEVIL: "Well, I suppose there was something to lie on. You are not laughing?"

EDDIE WILLERS, *still with the same strange eagerness, now listening with unexpected curiosity*: "Bravo! Well, is she lying there now?"

THE DEVIL: "That's the point, that she isn't. She lay there almost a thousand years and then she got up and went on."

EDDIE WILLERS, *laughing nervously and still seeming to be pondering something intently*: "What an ass! Does it make any difference whether she lies there forever or walks the quadrillion kilometers? It would take a billion years to walk it!"

THE DEVIL: "Much more than that. I haven't got a pencil and paper or I could work it out. But she got there long ago, and that's where the story begins."

EDDIE WILLERS: "What? She got there? But how did she get the billion years to do it?"

THE DEVIL: "Why, you keep thinking of our present earth! But our present earth may have been repeated a billion times. Why, it's become extinct, been frozen; cracked, broken to bits, disintegrated into its elements, again *the water above the firmament*, then again a comet, again a sun, again from the sun it becomes earth — and the same sequence may have been repeated endlessly and exactly the same to every detail, most unseemly and insufferably tedious..."

Transition to the Paradise...

Scene V — Delirium in Atlantis
"The Parable of the Onion"
"Atlas Shrugged" Part III – Chapter 1
"The Brothers Karamazov" Part III Book VII Chapter 3

Time: Eternity...

Place: A beautiful valley in heaven.

Cast: Ayn Rand,
    Prince Myshkin,
    Lebedev,
    An Elder Angel,
    A Host of Angels.

Summary: Not ready to accept an afterlife in the Atlantis, Ayn gains provisional admittance under the protection of Prince Myshkin, to allow her time to decide for herself if Paradise might be consistent with her principles.

ψ

Prince Myshkin steps forward to sponsor Ayn's entry to Paradise.

Angels, *in a general murmur:* "Yes, why? Why indeed?"

Prince Myshkin, *a voice from behind, simply, clearly:* "An act of charity."

Ayn, *offended, sarcastically:* "When people are unanimous, how does one man dare to dissent!"

Elder Angel, *authoritative, demanding:* "Who speaks!?"

Another Angel, *in happy surprise:* "It is Myshkin!"

ANOTHER ANGEL, *in astonishment, deference*: "...Prince Myshkin?"

PRINCE MYSHKIN, *pushing forward, states simply, clearly, decisively*: "An onion."

LEBEDEV: "Most Honorable Prince, it seems doubtful..." *trails off.*

AYN, *indignant*: "Guilt is a rope that wears thin!"

PRINCE MYSHKIN, *humbly yet unequivocally*: "Yes, you are credited with an act of altruism. The gift of an onion to a beggar woman."

AYN, *indignant*: "Idiot! I need no warrant for being, and no word of sanction upon my being. I am the warrant and sanction!"

PRINCE MYSHKIN, *not at all offended*: "Nonetheless, once, an onion."

AYN, *loosing control*: "What I am fighting is the idea that charity is no moral duty, no primary virtue!"

LEBEDEV: *with certainty that the Prince must be mistaken*: "Most Esteemed Prince, how can it be..." *trails off.*

PRINCE MYSHKIN: *simply, humbly*: "I'm afraid it's indisputable. An onion, once, given to a beggar, as a child."

AYN, *regaining control*: "I don't engage in charity..." *glancing hard at the Prince* "... and I don't gamble on incompetents."

AN ANGEL: "...Gamble?"

ANOTHER ANGEL: "...Incompetents?"

PRINCE MYSHKIN, *calmly*: "Inscribed in the book of life. An onion, a gift freely given."

AYN, *defiant*: "I never asked for faith, hope and charity, but always preferred facts, proof and profits!"

AN ANGEL, *eyebrows raised*: "...Proof?"

ANOTHER ANGEL, *surprised:* "...Profits?"

The Angels murmur.

AN ELDER ANGEL, *steps forward:* "This is all highly irregular, although the Prince is correct in asserting that a singular act of charity is sometimes sufficient grounds for entry, under sponsorship, provided it was given freely, in the spirit of charity."

AYN: "It was not out of pity or charity or any ugly reason like that!"

AN ANGEL, *eyebrows raised:* "...Pity?"

ANOTHER ANGEL, *surprised:* "...Charity?"

LEBEDEV, *astounded:* "Most Revered Prince... she is humiliated at a piece of charity!"

THE HOST OF ANGELS, *turning to Prince Myshkin:* "Well, how is it? Pity, Charity... or Spite?"

PRINCE MYSHKIN: "Let us consult the book of life, and each shall decide from himself..."

A You Tube video appears above. It is old Russia, mud, smoking burned-out hovels of homes, a destitute begging woman with a babe in arms reaches a pleading hand to a passing wagon. Young Ayn, a child, riding in the back of the wagon, sneaks an onion from the family stores and places it in the fugitive hand. The child Rand smiles in blessed contentment. Clearly an act of charity.

AYN, *in a fury:* "This is outrageous! You have just put me to a test in order to learn whether I'd once fallen to the lowest possible stage of altruism!"

LEBEDEV, *indignant:* "What foolishness, most well-bred Prince! ... that the theory that individual charity is useless!"

The Angels murmur.

AN ANGEL, *looking on the scene disapprovingly:* "An outrage!"

AN ELDER ANGEL, *decidedly:* "For this, she must be punished!"

THE HOST OF ON-LOOKING ANGELS, *in agreement:* "Here, Here!"

ELDER ANGEL: "Precedent is on the side of our brother, Prince Myshkin, an act of altruism cannot be erased from the book of life, for if the gift of a turnip or onion is discounted as insignificant, where shall the account begin?"

Rand is exasperated. Angels murmur in contention.

ELDER ANGEL: "However, our young sister will do well to walk off her arrogance."

AYN, *defiant:* "It is not a question of who is going to let me, but who is going to stop me!"

ELDER ANGEL: "No one will stop you. You'll find a service entrance just down the way; you may enter there..."

AYN: "Service entrance?"

ELDER ANGEL: "...a quadrillion kilometers down that road."

The Angels gasp.

AYN: "This evil is made possible by nothing but the sanction we give it!" *falls to the ground in protest.*

ψ

A hundred years pass. Rand still lies across the road, refusing to start. It is cold, she is sitting on a pile of wooden crates, muttering cursing. A passing angel sees she is shivering.

PASSING ANGEL: "Well, if you aren't going to walk, at least you should try to get warm..."

AYN, *defiant:* "How the hell am I going to do that?"

PASSING ANGEL: "I don't know, maybe you could build a fire..."

AYN: "With what?"

Act I Scene V

The passing angel produces an axe. It has been there all along.

Passing Angel: "Here, maybe you could use this..."

Ayn, *surprised:* "What is an axe doing here?" *spreads her arms to indicate the celestial expanse.*

The passing angel just shrugs as if to say, 'who's to know?' Ayn takes the axe.

ψ

A thousand years pass, Rand is still obstinate. A passing angel stops to offer her a drink of water from a canteen.

Passing Angel: "Aren't you going to get started? It's going to take awhile... I don't have a pencil and paper to work it out... more than a billion years, I should think..."

Ayn, *defiant:* "And where am I going to get a billion years?"

Passing Angel, *with pride and reverence:* "You'll be surprised how time flies by here. And there's so much to do! Why, the inventor of the great motor of the universe, don't you want to meet him?"

Ayn, *with sudden excitement:* "John!"

Passing Angel, *perplexed:* "John?"

Ayn, *lit up by a realization, mutters:* "I must find the inventor of that motor!"

Passing Angel, *perplexed:* "Who?"

Ayn, *triumphantly:* "Nothing is of any importance except that I must find him!"

Passing Angel, *doubtfully:* "John?"

Ayn: "John Galt!"

Passing Angel, *doubtfully:* "Who is John Galt?"

Ayn decides to get up, starts walking.

Transition to Eddie Willers' apartment...

Scene VI — Interview with the Destroyer
"Hosannah in the Highest"
"The Brothers Karamazov" Part IV Book XI Chapter 9

Time: Late one night...
Place: Eddie Willers' living room.
Cast: Eddie Willers and the Devil.

ψ

Eddie's interview with the Devil resumes...

Eddie Willers: "Well, well, what happened when she arrived?"

The Devil: "Why, the moment the gates of Paradise were open and she walked in; before she had been there two seconds, by her watch (though to my thinking her watch must have long dissolved into its elements on the way), she cried out that those two seconds were worth walking not a quadrillion kilometers but a quadrillion of quadrillions, raised to the quadrillionth power! In fact, she sang *hosannah* and overdid it so, that some persons there of lofty ideas wouldn't shake hands with her at first — she'd become too rapidly reactionary, they said. The Russian temperament. I repeat, it's a legend. I give it for what it's worth, so that's the sort of ideas we have on such subjects even now."

Transition to Paradise...

Scene VII — Delirium in Atlantis
"Listen Big Boy, if you wanna be a man..."
"Atlas Shrugged" Part III – Chapter 1
"The Brothers Karamazov" Part III Book VIII Chapter 8

Time: 30 billion years later...

Place: Service entrance of heaven.

Cast: Ayn Rand,
Guardian Angel,
Prince Myshkin,
Lebedev,
Eddie Willers.

Summary: Ayn finally arrives at the service entrance to heaven, where she is met by Prince Myshkin and Eddie Willers. They begin a quest to find the inventor of the motor.

ψ

Ayn arrives at the service entrance to heaven after hiking the quadrillion miles, out of breath. Finding the door locked, rings the bell. She shivers and hugs herself against the cold. She waits, then, exasperated, rings again.

GUARDIAN ANGEL, *opens the door, distastefully, in the manner of a butler*: "Yes..."

AYN, *indignant*: "I've come to see the inventor of the motor."

GUARDIAN ANGEL, *doubtfully, inquiringly*: "The motor?"

AYN: "The great motor of the universe!"

Guardian Angel: "Ah, yes, we heard you were coming..."

Ayn hugs herself against the cold, stomps her feet.

Ayn, *stepping inside the gate*: "Hosannah! Hosannah in the Highest!"

Guardian Angel, *pleased*: "Such enthusiasm!"

Ayn: "I would have walked quadrillion of quadrillions, raised to the quadrillionth power! Only to meet the inventor of the motor!"

An Angel, *disapprovingly*: "Reactionary!"

Another Angel, *sarcastically*: "Hosannah indeed!"

Ayn, *sarcastically, incredulously*: "The inventor of the motor, for God's sake! Take me to him!"

Prince Myshkin arrives.

Guardian Angel, *whispers to Prince Myshkin*: "There is something unusual about this case."

Prince Myshkin: "Yes, she is a gate crasher."

Guardian Angel, *surprised*: "Gate crasher?"

Prince Myshkin "She managed to crash land her plane into Paradise, no one knows quite how. She's not entirely sure she wants to be here... a scab, you might say."

Guardian Angel, *doubtfully*: "This is something we hadn't provided for, the first scab!"

Prince Myshkin, *handing over documents on a clipboard*: "Yes, yes, it's an unusual case, but you can see for yourself, all the paperwork is in order."

Guardian Angel, *sarcastically, bowing*: "Welcome to the kingdom of heaven."

Act I Scene VII

AYN: *looking to Prince Myshkin:* "Fool!"

Myshkin, not in the least offended, smiles, looks almost adoringly at Ayn. From a distance, approaching: singing, an old Negro spiritual, somewhat distant...

Workin' on the Railroad Line
(Key of F)

> *Listen Big Boy, if you wanna be a man,*
> *On the railroad line, on the railroad line...*
> *Swingin' Big Boy wid a hammer in yo' han'.*
> *Workin' on the railroad line.*
> *Workin' on the railroad line.*
> *Workin' on the railroad line.*

...growing louder

> *Listen Big Boy what I hear the people say*
> *On the railroad line. Yo' gal's goin' quit you*
> *'cause you never get no pay*
> *working on the railroad line.*

...appears, continues singing

> *Get you a gal like mine,*
> *Get you a gal like mine,*
> *Get you a gal like mine,*
> *Workin' on the railroad line.*

...the singer is Eddie Willers. He sees Ayn and the Prince.

EDDIE WILLERS, *thrilled:* "Dagny!"

AYN *coldly, correcting him:* "Ayn"

EDDIE WILLERS: "Dagny! Where you been! I stayed with the Comet to all the way to th' end!"

AYN: "Yes, I know, I left you there."

EDDIE WILLERS, *pleadingly:* "You left me there?"

AYN: "Yes, to show that, although you had virtue, you were lacking in the principles of a Mohammed or a Napoleon."

Eddie Willers, *despairing*: "Principles of a Napoleon?"

Ayn: *eagerly, desperately*: "Have you seen Hank? Where is John Galt?"

Eddie Willers, *shrugs*: "Ain't nobody knows fo' sure"

Ayn, *demanding*: "We must find them!"

Eddie Willers, *explaining*: "I know where your grandfather is…"

Ayn, *perplexed*: "…my grandfather?"

Eddie Willers, *excited*: "Old Nat Taggart, I think I know where he is…"

Ayn: "We must find him!"

Prince Myshkin: "Come Ayn, we'll look for them together!"

Ayn, *following Myshkin exclaims*: "Idiot!"

Transition to Eddie Willers' apartment…

Scene VIII — Interview with the Destroyer
"You'll kill me? No, excuse me, I will speak..."
"The Brothers Karamazov"
Part IV Book XI Chapter 9

Time: Late one night...

Place: Eddie Willers' living room.

Cast: Eddie Willers and the Devil.

Summary: The Destroyer describes the day when all men will unite.

ψ

Eddie Willers, *with an almost childish delight, as though he had succeeded in remembering something at last:* "I've caught you! That anecdote about the quadrillion years, I made up myself! I was seventeen then, I was at the high school. I made up that anecdote and told it to a schoolfellow called Korovkin, it was at Moscow... The anecdote is so characteristic that I couldn't have taken it from anywhere. I thought I'd forgotten it... but I've unconsciously recalled it — I recalled it myself — it was not you telling it! Thousands of things are unconsciously remembered like that even when people are being taken to execution... it's come back to me in a dream. You are that dream! You are a dream, not a living creature!"

The Devil, *pleased:* "From the vehemence with which you deny my existence, I am convinced that you believe in me."

Eddie Willers: "Not in the slightest! I haven't a hundredth part of a grain of faith in you!"

The Devil: "But you have the thousandth of a grain. Homeopathic doses perhaps are the strongest. Confess that you have faith even to the ten-thousandth of a grain."

EDDIE WILLERS, *furiously*: "Not for one minute!" (*then adds, strangely*) "but I should like to believe in you."

THE DEVIL: "Aha! There's an admission! But I am good-natured. I'll come to your assistance again. Listen, *it was I caught you*, not you me. I told you your anecdote which you'd forgotten, on purpose, so as to destroy your faith in me completely."

EDDIE WILLERS: "You are lying. The object of your visit is to convince me of your existence!"

THE DEVIL: "Just so. But hesitation, suspense, conflict between belief and disbelief — is sometimes such torture to a conscientious man, such as you are, that it's better to hang oneself at once. Knowing that you are inclined to believe in me, I administered some disbelief by telling you that anecdote. I lead you to belief and disbelief by turns, and I have my motive in it. It's the new method. As soon as you disbelieve in me completely, you'll begin assuring me to my face that I am not a dream but a reality. I know you. Then I shall have attained my object, which is an honorable one. I shall sow in you only a tiny grain of faith and it will grow into an oak-tree — and such an oak-tree that, sitting on it, you will long to enter the ranks of *the hermits in the wilderness and the saintly women*, for that is what you are secretly longing for. You'll dine on locusts, you'll wander into the wilderness to save your soul!"

EDDIE WILLERS: "Then it's for the salvation of my soul you are working, is it, you scoundrel?"

THE DEVIL: "One must do a good work sometimes. How ill-humored you are!"

EDDIE WILLERS: "*Fool!* Did you ever tempt those holy men who ate locusts and prayed seventeen years in the wilderness till they were overgrown with moss?"

THE DEVIL: "My dear fellow, I've done nothing else. One forgets the whole world and all the worlds, and sticks to one such saint, because he is a very precious diamond. One such soul, you know, is sometimes worth a whole constellation. We have our system of reckoning, you know. The conquest is priceless! And some of them, on my word, are not inferior to you in culture, though you won't believe it. They can contemplate such depths of belief and disbelief at the same moment that sometimes it really seems that they are within a hair's-breadth of being *turned upside down*, as the actor Gorbunov says."

EDDIE WILLERS: "Well, did you get your nose pulled?"

THE DEVIL, *observing sententiously*: "My dear fellow, it's better to get off with your nose pulled than without a nose at all. As an afflicted marquis observed not long ago (he must have been treated by a specialist) in confession to his spiritual father — a Jesuit. I was present, it was simply charming. *'Give me back my nose!'* he said, and he beat his breast. *'My son,'* said the priest evasively, *'all things are accomplished in accordance with the inscrutable decrees of Providence, and what seems a misfortune sometimes leads to extraordinary, though unapparent, benefits. If stern destiny has deprived you of your nose, it's to your advantage that no one can ever pull you by your nose.'* Replied the despairing marquis: *'Holy father, that's no comfort, I'd be delighted to have my nose pulled every day of my life, if it were only in its proper place.'* 'My son,' sighs the priest, *'you can't expect every blessing at once. This is murmuring against Providence, who even in this has not forgotten you, for if you repine as you repined just now, declaring you'd be glad to have your nose pulled for the rest of your life, your desire has already been fulfilled indirectly, for when you lost your nose, you were led by the nose."*

EDDIE WILLERS: "*Fool!* How stupid!"

THE DEVIL: "My dear friend, I only wanted to amuse you. But I swear that's the genuine Jesuit casuistry and I swear that it all happened word for word as I've told you. It happened lately and gave me a great deal of trouble. The unhappy young man shot himself that very night when he got home. I was by his side till the very last moment. Those Jesuit confessionals are really my most delightful diversion at melancholy moments. Here's another incident that happened only the other day. A little blonde Norman girl of twenty

— a buxom, unsophisticated beauty that would make your mouth water — comes to an old priest. She bends down and whispers her sin into the grating. 'Why, my daughter, have you fallen again already?' cries the priest: 'O Santa Maria, what do I hear! Not the same man this time, how long is this going on? Aren't you ashamed!' 'Ah, mon pere,' answers the sinner with tears of penitence, 'Ça lui fait tant de plaisir, et à moi si peu de peine!' *(Ah, my father, this gives him so much pleasure, and me so little pain!)* Fancy, such an answer! I drew back. It was the cry of nature, better than innocence itself, if you like. I absolved her sin on the spot and was turning to go, but I was forced to turn back. I heard the priest at the grating making an appointment with her for the evening — though he was an old man hard as flint, he fell in an instant! It was nature, the truth of nature asserted its rights! What? You are turning up your nose again? Angry again? I don't know how to please you..."

EDDIE WILLERS, *moaning miserably, helpless before his apparition:* "Leave me alone, you are beating on my brain like a haunting nightmare. I am bored with you, agonizingly and insufferably. I would give anything to be able to shake you off!"

THE DEVIL: "I repeat, moderate your expectations, don't demand of me *everything great and noble,* and you'll see how well we shall get on. You are really angry with me for not having appeared to you in a red glow, with thunder and lightning, with scorched wings, but have shown myself in such a modest form. You are wounded, in the first place, in your aesthetic feelings, and, secondly, in your pride. How could such a vulgar devil visit such a great man as you! Yes, there is that romantic strain in you, that was so derided by Byelinsky. I can't help it, young man, as I got ready to come to you I did think as a joke of appearing in the figure of a retired general who had served in the Caucasus, with a star of the Lion and the Sun on my coat. But I was positively afraid of doing it, for you'd have thrashed me for daring to pin the Lion and the Sun on my coat, instead of, at least, the Polar Star or the Sirius. And you keep on saying I am stupid, but, mercy on us! I make no claim to be equal to you in intelligence. Mephistopheles declared to Faust that he desired evil, but did only good. Well, he can say what he likes, it's quite the opposite with me. I am perhaps the one man in

Act I Scene VIII

all creation who loves the truth and genuinely desires good. I was there when the Word, Who died on the Cross, rose up into heaven bearing on His bosom the soul of the penitent thief. I heard the glad shrieks of the cherubim singing and shouting hosannah and the thunderous rapture of the seraphim which shook heaven and all creation, and I swear to you by all that's sacred, I longed to join the choir and shout hosannah with them all. The word had almost escaped me, had almost broken from my lips... you know how susceptible and aesthetically impressionable I am. But common sense — oh, a most unhappy trait in my character — kept me in due bounds and I let the moment pass! For what would have happened, I reflected, what would have happened after my hosannah? Everything on earth would have been extinguished at once and no events could have occurred. And so, solely from a sense of duty and my social position, was forced to suppress the good moment and to stick to my nasty task. Somebody takes all the credit of what's good for Himself, and nothing but nastiness is left for me. But I don't envy the honor of a life of idle imposture, I am not ambitious. Why am I, of all creatures in the world, doomed to be cursed by all decent people and even to be kicked, for if I put on mortal form I am bound to take such consequences sometimes? I know, of course, there's a secret in it, but they won't tell me the secret for anything, for then perhaps, seeing the meaning of it, I might bawl hosannah, and the indispensable minus would disappear at once, and good sense would reign supreme throughout the whole world. And that, of course, would mean the end of everything, even of magazines and newspapers, for who would take them in? I know that at the end of all things I shall be reconciled. I, too, shall walk my quadrillion and learn the secret. But till that happens I am sulking and fulfill my destiny though it's against the grain — that is, to ruin thousands for the sake of saving one. How many souls have had to be ruined and how many honorable reputations destroyed for the sake of that one righteous man, Job, over whom they made such a fool of me in old days! Yes, till the secret is revealed, there are two sorts of truths for me — one, their truth, yonder, which I know nothing about so far, and the other my own. And there's no knowing which will turn out the better... Are you asleep?"

Eddie Willers, *groaning angrily*: "I might well be! All my stupid ideas—outgrown, thrashed out long ago, and flung aside like a dead carcass you present to me as something new!"

THE DEVIL: "There's no pleasing you! And I thought I should fascinate you by my literary style. That hosannah in the skies really wasn't bad, was it? And then that ironical tone *a la Heine*, eh?"

EDDIE WILLERS: "No, I was never such a flunky! How then could my soul beget a flunky like you?"

THE DEVIL: "My dear fellow, I know a most charming and attractive young Russian gentleman, a young thinker and a great lover of literature and art, the author of a promising poem entitled *The Grand Inquisitor*. I was only thinking of him!"

EDDIE WILLERS, *crimson with shame*: "I forbid you to speak of *The Grand Inquisitor!*"

THE DEVIL: "And the *Geological Cataclysm*. Do you remember? That was a poem, now!"

EDDIE WILLERS: "Hold your tongue, or I'll kill you!"

THE DEVIL: "You'll kill me? No, excuse me, I will speak. I came to treat myself to that pleasure. Oh, I love the dreams of my ardent young friends, quivering with eagerness for life! *There are new men,* you decided last spring, when you were meaning to come here, *they propose to destroy everything and begin with cannibalism.* Stupid fellows! they didn't ask my advice! I maintain that nothing need be destroyed, that we only need to destroy the idea of God in man, that's how we have to set to work. It's that, that we must begin with. Oh, blind race of men who have no understanding! As soon as men have all of them denied God — and I believe that period, analogous with geological periods, will come to pass — the old conception of the universe will fall of itself without cannibalism, and, what's more, the old morality, and everything will begin anew. Men will unite to take from life all it can give, but only for joy and happiness in the present world. Man will be lifted up with a spirit of divine Titanic pride and the man-god will appear. From hour to hour extending his conquest of nature infinitely by his will and his science, man will feel such lofty joy from hour to hour in doing it that it will make up for all his old dreams of the joys of heaven. Everyone will know that he is mortal and will accept death proudly and serenely like a god. His pride will teach him that it's useless for him to repine at life's being a moment, and he will love his brother without need of reward. Love will be sufficient only for a moment of life, but the very consciousness of its momentariness will intensify its fire, which now is dissipated in dreams of eternal love beyond the grave... and so on and so on in the same style. Charming!"

Eddie sits with his eyes on the floor, and his hands pressed to his ears, but he begins trembling all over.

THE DEVIL, *continues:* "The question now is, (my young thinker reflected), is it possible that such a period will ever come? If it does, everything is determined and humanity is settled for ever. But as, owing to man's inveterate stupidity, this cannot come about for at least a thousand years, everyone who recognizes the truth even now may legitimately order his life as he pleases, on the new principles. In that sense, *all things are lawful* for him. What's more, even if this period never comes to pass, since there is anyway no God and no immortality, the new man may well become the man-god, even if he is the only one in the whole world, and promoted to his new position, he may lightheartedly overstep all the barriers of the old morality of the old slave man, if necessary. There is no law for God. Where God stands, the place is holy. Where I stand will be at once the foremost place... *all things are lawful* and that's the end of it! That's all very charming; but if you want to swindle why do you want a moral sanction for doing it? But that's our investment banker all over. He can't bring himself to swindle without a moral sanction. He is so in love with truth..."

Act II
The Police Inspector

"I am ready to bow down to them, of course, but you must admit it's alarming if there are a great many of them, eh?"

Scene I — Second Eddie
"it ain't never no worry t' her..."

"Atlas Shrugged"
Part II Chapter 7

Time: Late at night...

Place: In the Taggart Terminal underground cafeteria.

Cast: Eddie Willers.

Summary: Eddie Willers carries on a one-sided conversation with an unseen figure.

ψ

We hear only Eddie Willers' side of the conversation...

Eddie Willers: "Do you take it seriously if somebody tells you that a meteor is going to destroy the earth?"

a momentary pause...

Eddie Willers: "I don't either..."

a pause as Eddie listens...

Eddie Willers: "*From Ocean to Ocean forever* – that's what we heard all through our childhood, she and I."

a pause...

Eddie Willers: "No, they didn't say *forever*, but that's what it meant..."

a brief pause...

EDDIE WILLERS: "You know, I'm not any kind of great man. I couldn't have built that railroad. If it goes, I won't be able to bring it back. I'll have to go with it..."

...another pause...

EDDIE WILLERS: "Don't pay any attention to me, I don't know why I should want to say things like that... guess I'm just a little tired tonight."

almost right away...

EDDIE WILLERS: "...Yes, I worked late. She didn't ask me to stay, but there was a light on under her door, long after the others had gone..."

a brief pause...

EDDIE WILLERS: "Yes, she's gone home by now..."

a bit longer as Eddie listens...

EDDIE WILLERS: "Trouble? Oh, der's always trouble in da office, but it ain't never no worry t' her..."

Eddie begins singing:

A Little Talk with Dagny
—*to the tune of "A Little Talk with Jesus" (Key of F)*

*O' a little talk with Dagny makes it right, all right,
little talk with Dagny makes it right all right.
Troubles of ev'ry kind, Thank God I'll always find,
that a little talk with Dagny makes it right.*

*My brother, I remember when Jim Taggart was the boss,
I cried "Have mercy, Dagny", but my soul was tossed.
Till I heard Dagny Taggart say "Come here, I'll show the way!"
And a little talk with Dagny makes it right.*

*O' a little talk with Dagny makes it right, all right,
little talk with Dagny makes it right all right.
Troubles of ev'ry kind, Thank God I'll always find,
that a little talk with Dagny makes it right.*

*Sometimes the forked lightning and muttering thunder, too
of trials and tribulations make it hard for me and you.
But Dagny is our friend, she'll keep us to the end;
And a little talk with Dagny makes it right.*

*O' a little talk with Dagny makes it right, all right,
little talk with Dagny makes it right all right.
Troubles of ev'ry kind, Thank God I'll always find,
that a little talk with Dagny makes it right.*

Transition to the interview with the police inspector...

Scene II — Interview with the Police Inspector
"The New Jerusalem"
"Crime and Punishment" Part III Chapter 5
"Atlas Shrugged" Part I Chapter 3

Time: Afternoon...

Place: Office of police inspector Pytor Petrovich.

Cast: Police Inspector Pytor Petrovich,
  Nat Taggart as Rodion Romanovitch Raskolnikov,
  Eddie Willers as Razumihin,
  Prince Myshkin,
  Ayn Rand.

Summary: Police Inspector Pytor Petrovich leads a discussion with Nathaniel Taggart on his theory of criminal psychology.

ψ

In a comfortable studio policy inspector Porfiry Petrovitch, Nat Taggart with his companion, Eddie Willers. Prince Myshkin ushers in Rand. They seat themselves on the sofa and the conversation ensues...

Porfiry Petrovitch, *to Nat Taggart*: "There is, if you recollect, a suggestion that there are certain persons who can... that is, not precisely are able to, but have a perfect right to commit breaches of morality and crimes, and that the law is not for them."

Nat Taggart smiles at the exaggerated and intentional distortion of his idea.

Eddie Willers, *with alarm*: "What? What do you mean? A right to crime? But not because of the influence of environment?"

PORFIRY PETROVITCH: "No, not exactly because of it, in his article all men are divided into *ordinary* and *extraordinary*. Ordinary men have to live in submission, have no right to transgress the law, because, don't you see, they are ordinary. But *extraordinary* men have a right to commit any crime and to transgress the law in any way, just because they are extraordinary. That was your idea, if I am not mistaken?"

EDDIE WILLERS, *muttering in bewilderment*: "What do you mean? That can't be right?"

Nat Taggart, smiling again, sees the point at once, and knows where Porfiry Petrovich wants to drive him. He decides to take up the challenge.

NAT TAGGART, *simply and modestly:* "That wasn't quite my contention, yet I admit that you have stated it almost correctly; perhaps, if you like, perfectly so." (*It almost gives him pleasure to admit this.*) "The only difference is that I don't contend that extraordinary people are always bound to commit breaches of morals, as you call it. In fact, I doubt whether such an argument could be published. I simply hinted that an *extraordinary* man has the right — that is not an official right, but an inner right to decide in his own conscience to overstep — certain obstacles, and only in case it is essential for the practical fulfillment of his idea (sometimes, perhaps, of benefit to the whole of humanity). You say that my article isn't definite; I am ready to make it as clear as I can. Perhaps I am right in thinking you want me to; very well. I maintain that if the discoveries of Kepler and Newton could not have been made known except by sacrificing the lives of one, a dozen, a hundred, or more men, Newton would have had the right, would indeed have been duty bound... to *eliminate* the dozen or the hundred men for the sake of making his discoveries known to the whole of humanity. But it does not follow from that that Newton had a right to murder people right and left and to steal every day in the market. Then, I remember, I maintain in my article that all... well, legislators and leaders of men, such as Lycurgus, Solon, Mohammed, Napoleon, and so on, were all without exception criminals, from the very fact that, making a new law, they transgressed the ancient one, handed down from their ancestors and held sacred by the people, and they did not

Act II Scene II

stop short at bloodshed either, if that bloodshed — often of innocent persons fighting bravely in defense of ancient law — were of use to their cause. It's remarkable, in fact, that the majority, indeed, of these benefactors and leaders of humanity were guilty of terrible carnage. In short, I maintain that all great men or even men a little out of the common, that is to say, those capable of giving some new word, must from their very nature be criminals — more or less, of course. Otherwise it's hard for them to get out of the common rut; and to remain in the common rut is what they can't submit to, from their very nature again, and to my mind they ought not, indeed, to submit to it. You see that there is nothing particularly new in all that. The same thing has been printed and read a thousand times before. As for my division of people into *ordinary* and *extraordinary*, I acknowledge that it's somewhat arbitrary, but I don't insist upon exact numbers. I only believe in my leading idea that men are *in general* divided by a law of nature into two categories, inferior (ordinary), that is, so to say, material that serves only to reproduce its kind, and men who have the gift or the talent to utter *a new word*. There are, of course, innumerable sub-divisions, but the distinguishing features of both categories are fairly well marked. The first category, generally speaking, are men conservative in temperament and law-abiding; they live under control and love to be controlled. To my thinking it is their duty to be controlled, because that's their vocation, and there is nothing humiliating in it for them. The second category all transgress the law; they are *destroyers* or disposed to destruction according to their capacities. The crimes of these men are of course relative and varied; for the most part they seek in very varied ways the destruction of the present for the sake of the better. But if such a one is forced for the sake of his idea to step over a corpse or wade through blood, he can, I maintain, find within himself, in his conscience, a sanction for wading through blood — that depends on the idea and its dimensions, note that. It's only in that sense I speak of their right to crime in my article (you remember it began with the legal question). There's no need for such anxiety, however; the masses will scarcely ever admit this right, they punish them or hang them (more or less), and in doing so fulfill quite justly their conservative vocation. But the same masses set these criminals on a pedestal in the next generation and worship them (more or less). The first category is always the man of the present, the second the man of the future. The first preserve the world and people it, the second move the world and lead it to its goal. Each class has an equal right to exist. In fact, all have equal rights with me — and *vive la guerre éternelle* — till the New Jerusalem, of course!"

Porfiry Petrovitch: "Then you believe in the New Jerusalem, do you?"

Nat Taggart, *firmly, but keeping his eyes fixed to a spot on the floor*: "I do."

Porfiry Petrovitch: "And... and do you believe in God? Excuse my curiosity."

Nat Taggart, *raising his eyes to Porfiry, repeats*: "I do."

Porfiry Petrovitch: "And... do you believe in Lazarus' rising from the dead?"

Nat Taggart, *stammers*: "I... I do. Why do you ask all this?"

Porfiry Petrovitch: "You believe it literally?"

Nat Taggart: "Literally."

Porfiry Petrovitch: "You don't say so... I asked from curiosity. Excuse me. But let us go back to the question; they are not always executed. Some, on the contrary..."

Nat Taggart: "Triumph in their lifetime? Oh, yes, some attain their ends in this life, and then..."

Porfiry Petrovitch: "They begin executing other people?"

Nat Taggart: "If it's necessary; indeed, for the most part they do. Your remark is very witty."

Porfiry Petrovitch: "Thank you. But tell me this: how do you distinguish those extraordinary people from the ordinary ones? Are there signs at their birth? I feel there ought to be more exactitude, more external definition. Excuse the natural anxiety of a practical law-abiding citizen, but couldn't they adopt a special uniform, for instance, couldn't they wear something, be branded in some way? For you know if confusion arises and a member of one category imagines that he belongs to the other, begins to *eliminate obstacles* as you so happily expressed it, then…"

NAT TAGGART: "Oh, that very often happens! That remark is wittier than the other."

PORFIRY PETROVITCH: "Thank you."

NAT TAGGART: "No reason to; but take note that the mistake can only arise in the first category, that is among the ordinary people (as I perhaps unfortunately called them). In spite of their predisposition to obedience very many of them, through a playfulness of nature, sometimes vouchsafed even to the cow, like to imagine themselves advanced people, *destroyers*, and to push themselves into the *new movement*, and this quite sincerely. Meanwhile the *really* new people are very often unobserved by them, or even despised as reactionaries of groveling tendencies. But I don't think there is any considerable danger here, and you really need not be uneasy for they never go very far. Of course, they might have a thrashing sometimes for letting their fancy run away with them and to teach them their place, but no more; in fact, even this isn't necessary as they castigate themselves, for they are very conscientious: some perform this service for one another and others chastise themselves with their own hands… They will impose various public acts of penitence upon themselves with a beautiful and edifying effect; in fact you've nothing to be uneasy about… it's a law of nature."

PORFIRY PETROVITCH: "Well, you have certainly set my mind more at rest on that score; but there's another thing that worries me. Tell me, please, are there many people who have the right to kill others, these *extraordinary* people? I am ready to bow down to them, of course, but you must admit it's alarming if there are a great many of them, eh?"

Nat Taggart, *continuing in the same tone*: "Oh, you needn't worry about that either. People with new ideas, people with the faintest capacity for saying something *new*, are extremely few in number, extraordinarily so in fact. One thing only is clear, that the appearance of all these grades and sub-divisions of men must follow with unfailing regularity some law of nature. That law, of course, is unknown at present, but I am convinced that it exists, and one day may become known. The vast mass of mankind is mere material, and only exists in order by some great effort, by some mysterious process, by means of some crossing of races and stocks, to bring into the world at last perhaps one man out of a thousand with a spark of independence. One in ten thousand perhaps — I speak roughly, approximately — is born with some independence, and with still greater independence one in a hundred thousand. The man of genius is one of millions, and the great geniuses, the crown of humanity, appear on earth perhaps one in many thousand millions. In fact I have not peeped into the retort in which all this takes place. But there certainly is and must be a definite law, it cannot be a matter of chance."

Eddie Willers, *unable to contain himself*: "Why, are you both joking? There you sit, making fun of one another. Are you serious, Mr. Taggart?"

> Nat Taggart raises his pale and almost mournful face and makes no reply. The unconcealed, persistent, nervous, and discourteous sarcasm of Porfiry seems strange to Eddie Willers beside that quiet and mournful face.

Eddie Willers: "Well, sir, if you are really serious... you are right, of course, in saying that it's not new, that it's like what we've read and heard a thousand times already; but what is really original in all this, and is exclusively your own, to my horror, is that you sanction bloodshed *in the name of conscience*, and, excuse my saying so, with such fanaticism... That, I take it, is the point of your article. But that sanction of bloodshed *by conscience* is to my mind... more terrible than the official, legal sanction of bloodshed..."

Porfiry Petrovitch: "You are quite right, it is more terrible."

Eddie Willers: "Yes, you must have exaggerated! There is some mistake, I shall read it. You can't think that! I shall read it."

Nat Taggart: "All that is not in the article, there's only a hint of it."

Porfiry Petrovitch, *unable to sit still*: "Yes, yes. Your attitude to crime is pretty clear to me now, but... excuse me for my impertinence (I am really ashamed to be worrying you like this), you see, you've removed my anxiety as to the two grades getting mixed, but... there are various practical possibilities that make me uneasy! What if some man or youth imagines that he is a Lycurgus or Mohammed — a future one of course — and suppose he begins to remove all obstacles... He has some great enterprise before him and needs money for it... and tries to get it... do you see?"

Nat Taggart, *calmly*: "I must admit, that such cases certainly must arise. The vain and foolish are particularly apt to fall into that snare; young people especially."

Porfiry Petrovitch: "Yes, you see. Well then?"

Nat Taggart, *in reply*: "What then? That's not my fault. So it is and so it always will be. He said just now" (*nods at Eddie Willers*) "that I sanction bloodshed. Society is too well protected by prisons, banishment, criminal investigators, penal servitude. There's no need to be uneasy. You have but to catch the thief."

Porfiry Petrovitch: "And what if we do catch him?"

Nat Taggart: "Then he gets what he deserves."

Porfiry Petrovitch: "You are certainly logical. But what of his conscience?"

Nat Taggart: "Why do you care about that?"

Porfiry Petrovitch: "Simply from humanity."

Nat Taggart: "If he has a conscience he will suffer for his mistake. That will be his punishment — as well as the prison."

Eddie Willers, *frowning:* "But the real geniuses, those who have the right to murder? Oughtn't they to suffer at all even for the blood they've shed?"

Nat Taggart: "Why the word *ought*? It's not a matter of permission or prohibition. He will suffer if he is sorry for his victim. Pain and suffering are always inevitable for a large intelligence and a deep heart."

Nat Taggart, *dreamily, not in the tone of the conversation:* "The really great men must, I think, have great sadness on earth."

> *He raises his eyes, looks earnestly at them all, smiles, and takes off his cap. Everyone gets up.*

Porfiry Petrovitch: "Well, you may abuse me, be angry with me if you like, but I can't resist. Allow me one little question (I know I am troubling you). There is just one little notion I want to express, simply that I may not forget it."

Nat Taggart, *stands waiting, pale and grave:* "Very good, tell me your little notion..."

Porfiry Petrovitch: "Well, you see... I really don't know how to express it properly... It's a playful, psychological idea... When you were writing your article, surely you couldn't have helped, he-he! Fancying yourself... just a little, an *extraordinary* man, uttering a *new word* in your sense. That's so, isn't it?"

Nat Taggart, *contemptuously:* "Quite possibly."

> *Eddie Willers moves nervously.*

Porfiry Petrovitch: "And, if so, could you bring yourself in case of worldly difficulties and hardship or for some service to humanity — to overstep obstacles? For instance, to rob and murder?"

> *And again he winks with his left eye, and laughs noiselessly just as before.*

Nat Taggart, *defiantly and haughty contempt:* "If I did I certainly should not tell you."

Act II Scene II

Porfiry Petrovitch: "No, I was only interested on account of your article, from a literary point of view..."

Nat Taggart, *dryly*: "Allow me to observe, that I don't consider myself a Mohammed or a Napoleon, nor any personage of that kind, and not being one of them I cannot tell you how I should act."

Porfiry Petrovitch, *with alarming familiarity*: "Oh, come, don't we all think ourselves Napoleons now?"

Ayn: *suddenly:* "Excuse me, if I've heard you right, crime must not only be permitted but even recognized as the inevitable and the most rational outcome for a Mohammed or a Napoleon! Is that so or not?"

Nat Taggart: "Quite so."

Ayn: "I'll remember it."

Having uttered these words Ayn ceases speaking as suddenly as she had begun. Everyone looks at her with curiosity.

Act III
The Wormwood Star

"My conclusion is vast!"

Scene I - Third Eddie

"Is there every any reason to be afraid?"

"Atlas Shrugged"
Part I Chapter 3

Time: Late at night...

Place: In the Taggart Rail underground cafeteria.

Cast: Eddie Willers.

Summary: Eddie Willers carries on a one-sided conversation with an unseen figure.

ψ

Only Eddie Willers' side of the conversation can be heard.

Eddie Willers: "I feel like a fugitive."

Eddie Willers: "I guess you know why I haven't been here for months..."

listens...

Eddie Willers: "I'm supposed to be vice president now."

listens...

Eddie Willers: "The vice president in charge of operations..."

listens...

Eddie Willers: "For God's sake, don't take it seriously."

listens...

Eddie Willers: "I stood it for as long as I could, and then I had to escape, if only for one evening... the first time I came down here for dinner, after my alleged promotion, they all stared at me so much, I didn't come back. Well, let them stare. You don't. I'm glad it doesn't make any difference to you..."

listens...

EDDIE WILLERS: "No, I haven't seen her for two weeks, but I speak to her on the phone every day, sometimes twice a day."

listens...

EDDIE WILLERS: "Yes, I know how she feels, she loves it. What is it we hear over the telephone — sound vibrations, isn't it? Well, her voice sounds as if it were turning into light vibrations — if you know what I mean. She enjoys running that horrible battle single-handed and winning..."

listens...

EDDIE WILLERS: "Oh yes, she's winning! Do you know why you haven't read anything about the *John Galt Line* in the newspapers for some time? Because it's going so well..."

listens...

EDDIE WILLERS: "...Only..." *pauses* "...that Rearden Metal rail will be the greatest track ever built, but what will be the use if we don't have any engines powerful enough to take advantage of it? Look at the kind of patched coal-burners we've got left — they can barely manage to drag themselves fast enough for old trolley-car rails..."

listens...

EDDIE WILLERS: "Still, there's hope The United Locomotive Works went bankrupt. That's the best break we've had in the last few weeks, because their plant has been bought by Dwight Sanders. He's a brilliant engineer who's got the only good aircraft plant in the country. He had to sell the aircraft plant to his brother in order to take over the United Locomotive. That's on account of the Equalization of Opportunity Bill."

listens...

EDDIE WILLERS: "Sure it's just a setup between them, but can you blame him? Anyway, we'll be seeing Diesels coming out of the United Locomotive Works now. Dwight Sanders will start things going..."

listens...

EDDIE WILLERS: "...Yes, she's counting on him. Why do you ask?"

listens...

EDDIE WILLERS: "...Yes, he's crucially important to us right now. We've just signed a contract with him, for the first ten Diesel engines he'll build. When I phoned her that the contract was signed, she laughed and said, 'You see, is there every any reason to be afraid?'"

transition to Prince Myshkin's Villa...

Scene II — Of Railways

"What, these wagons may coldly exclude?"

"The Idiot"
Part III Chapter 4

Time: Shortly before dawn of a very short night...

Place: At Prince Myshkin's Villa just outside the gates of heaven.

Cast: Lebedev,
Prince Myshkin,
Eddie Willers as Nikolai Ardalyonovitch Ivolgin (Kolya),
Bertram Scudder as Gavril Ardalyonovich Ivolgin (Gayna),
Mr. Thompson as General Ivolgin,
Johnnie Dawes as Hippolyte,
Wesley Mouch as Keller,
Ayn Rand,
Francisco d'Anconia,
Ragnar Danneskjöld,
John Galt,
a host of revelers.

Summary: A party to celebrate the reunion of Ayn with her Ideal Men, at Prince Myshkin's Villa just outside the gates of heaven. Francisco, Ragnar and John Galt arrive, preceded by a warning from Lebedev. Drinks and revelry follow. In the ensuing conversation, Lebedev is called upon to defend is interpretation of the Wormwood Star of the Apocalypse.

ψ

At a party at Prince Myshkin's Villa in heaven. Talking and laughing. Ayn is dancing a triumphant jig alone to an old phonograph recording of a 'Marionettes at Midnight', pivoting her finger to the center of her head as she does pirouettes. She takes up a baton and pretends to conduct the orchestra, triumphantly.

A gospel trio entertains the revelers, singing:

O It's Goin' to be a Mighty Day
(Key of F)

O it's goin' to be a mighty day,
O it's goin' to be a mighty day,
O it's goin' to be a mighty day,
O it's goin' to be a mighty day.

Yes the book of Revelations to be brought forth on that day
An ev'ry leaf unfolded the book of seven seals.

Chorus

The good ol' train she be passin' by
She jarred the earth an' shook the sky

Chorus

She's a loaded down with wheat and corn
She might juz pass you by, pass you by.

Chorus

Ganya, Lebedev and Prince Myshkin stand admiring Ayn. The arrival of guests is announced.

GANYA, *turning to Lebedev, inquires about the guests:* "They are Nihilists, are they not?"

LEBEDEV, *very excited:* "No, they are not Nihilists, this is another lot — a special group, according to my nephew they are more advanced even than the Nihilists." *(turning to Prince Myshkin)* "You are quite wrong, excellency, if you think that your presence will intimidate them; nothing intimidates them. Educated men, learned men even, are to be found among Nihilists; these go further, in that they are *men of action*. The movement is, properly speaking, a derivative from Nihilism — though they are only known indi-

Act III Scene II

rectly, and by hearsay, for they never advertise their doings in the papers. They go straight to the point. For them, it is not a question of showing that Pushkin is stupid, or that Russia must be torn in pieces. No; but if they have a great desire for anything, they believe they have a right to get it even at the cost of the lives, say, of eight persons. They are checked by no obstacles. In fact, Prince, I should not advise you…"

> *Despite the warning, Prince Myshkin rises, and makes his way to open the door for his visitors. Ragnar Danneskjöld, Francisco d'Anconia and John Galt come in together. A joyous reunion ensues, as Ayn calls out their names in turn, as they embrace. They call her 'Dagny'; she does not object.*

JOHNNIE DAWES: "Do you know I am specially glad that today is your birthday!"

PRINCE MYSHKIN: "Why?"

JOHNNIE DAWES: "You'll soon see. D'you know I had a feeling that there would be a lot of people here tonight? It's not the first time that my presentiments have been fulfilled. I wish I had known it was your birthday, I'd have brought you a present — perhaps I have got a present for you! Who knows? Ha, ha! How long is it now before daylight?"

SOMEONE, *looking at his watch*: "Not a couple of hours."

SOMEONE ELSE: "What's the good of daylight now? One can read all night in the open air without it."

JOHNNIE DAWES: "The good of it! Well, I want just to see a ray of the sun. Can one drink to the sun's health, do you think, Prince?"

PRINCE MYSHKIN: "Oh, I dare say one can; but you had better be calm and lie down."

JOHNNIE DAWES: "You are always preaching about resting; you are a regular nurse to me, Prince. As soon as the sun begins to *resound* in the sky — what poet said that? 'The sun resounded in the sky.' It is beautiful, though there's no sense in it! — then we will go to bed. Lebedev, tell me, is the sun the source of life? What does the source, or *spring*, of life really mean in the Apocalypse? You have heard of the 'Star that is called *Wormwood*' Prince?"

PRINCE MYSHKIN: "I have heard that Lebedev explains it as the railroads that cover Europe like a net."

Everybody laughs, and Lebedev gets up abruptly.

LEBEDEV, *waving his hands to impose silence*: "No! Allow me, that is not what we are discussing! Allow me! With these gentlemen... all these gentlemen..."

LEBEDEV, *suddenly addressing Prince Myshkin*: "On certain points... that is..." (*thumps the table repeatedly, laughter all around*).

LEBEDEV, *evincing a supreme contempt for his opponents*: "It is not right! Half an hour ago, Prince, it was agreed among us that no one should interrupt, no one should laugh, that each person was to express his thoughts freely; and then at the end, when everyone had spoken, objections might be made, even by the atheists. We chose Mr. Thompson as president. Now without some such rule and order, anyone might be shouted down, even in the loftiest and most profound thought..."

SOMEONE: "Go on! Go on! Nobody is going to interrupt you!"

SOMEONE ELSE: "Speak, but keep to the point!"

ANOTHER: "What is this *star*?"

MR. THOMPSON, *with much gravity*: "I have no idea."

WESLEY MOUCH, *a little drunk*: "I love these arguments, Prince, scientific and political."

WESLEY MOUCH, *turning suddenly towards Bertram Scudder*: "Do you know, I simply adore reading the accounts of the debates in the English parliament. Not that the discussions themselves interest me; I am not a politician, you know; but it delights me to see how they address each other '*the noble lord who agrees with me,*' '*my honourable opponent who astonished Europe with his proposal,*'

Act III Scene II

'*the noble viscount sitting opposite*' — all these expressions, all this parliamentarianism of a free people, has an enormous attraction for me. It fascinates me, Prince. I have always been an artist in the depths of my soul, I assure you."

BERTRAM SCUDDER, *in high spirits, his gaiety was mingled with triumph, only meaning to egg him on, but he grows excited himself at the same time*: "Do you mean to say, do you mean to say that railways are accursed inventions, that they are a source of ruin to humanity, a poison poured upon the earth to corrupt the springs of life?"

LEBEDEV, *with a mixture of violent anger and extreme enjoyment*: "Not the railways, oh dear, no! Considered alone, the railways will not pollute the springs of life, but as a whole they are accursed. The whole tendency of our latest centuries, in its scientific and materialistic aspect, is most probably accursed."

BERTRAM SCUDDER: "Is it certainly accursed? Or do you only mean it might be? That is an important point!"

LEBEDEV, *vehemently*: "It is accursed, certainly accursed!"

SOMEONE, *smiling*: "Don't go so fast, Lebedev; you are much milder in the morning."

LEBEDEV, *earnestly*: "But, on the other hand, more frank in the evening! In the evening sincere and frank, more candid, more exact, more honest, more honourable, and... although I may show you my weak side, I challenge you all; you atheists, for instance! How are you going to save the world? How find a straight road of progress, you men of science, of industry, of cooperation, of trade unions, and all the rest? How are you going to save it, I say? By what? By credit? What is credit? To what will credit lead you?"

BERTRAM SCUDDER: "You are too inquisitive."

LEBEDEV: "Well, anyone who does not interest himself in questions such as this is, in my opinion, a mere fashionable dummy."

BERTRAM SCUDDER: "But it will lead at least to solidarity, and balance of interests, you will reach that with nothing to help you but credit? Without recourse to any moral principle, having for your foundation only individual selfishness, and the satisfaction of material desires? Universal peace, and the happiness of mankind as a whole, being the result! Is it really so that I may understand you, sir?"

BERTRAM SCUDDER, *now thoroughly roused:* "But the universal necessity of living, of drinking, of eating — in short, the whole scientific conviction that this necessity can only be satisfied by universal cooperation and the solidarity of interests — is, it seems to me, a strong enough idea to serve as a basis, so to speak, and a *spring of life* for humanity in future centuries."

LEBEDEV: "The necessity of eating and drinking, that is to say, solely the instinct of self-preservation... Is not that enough? The instinct of self-preservation is the normal law of humanity..."

BERTRAM SCUDDER, *breaking in:* "Who told you that?"

LEBEDEV: "It is a law, doubtless, but a law neither more nor less normal than that of destruction, even self-destruction. Is it possible that the whole normal law of humanity is contained in this sentiment of self-preservation?"

JOHNNIE DAWES, *turning towards Bertram Scudder and looking at him with a queer sort of curiosity:* "Ah!"

> Then seeing that Bertram Scutter was laughing, he began to laugh himself, nudged Eddie, who was sitting beside him, with his elbow.

JOHNNIE DAWES, *again, cries out:* "What time is it!"

> He pulls Eddie's silver watch out of his hand, and looks at it eagerly. Then, as if he had forgotten everything, he stretches himself out on the sofa, put his hands behind his head, and looked up at the sky. After a moment he gets up and comes back to the table to listen to Lebedev's outpourings, as the latter passionately comments on Bertram Scudder's paradox.

BERTRAM SCUDDER: "That is an artful and traitorous idea. A smart notion, thrown out as an apple of discord. But it is just. You are a

Act III Scene II

scoffer, a man of the world, a cavalry officer, and, though not without brains, you do not realize how profound is your thought, nor how true. Yes, the laws of self-preservation and of self-destruction are equally powerful in this world. The Devil will hold his empire over humanity until a limit of time which is still unknown."

LEBEDEV: "You laugh? You do not believe in the Devil? Scepticism as to the Devil is a French idea, and it is also a frivolous one. Do you know who the Devil is? Do you know his name? Although you don't know his name you make a mockery of his form, following the example of Voltaire. You sneer at his hoofs, at his tail, at his horns — all of them the product of your imagination! In reality the Devil is a great and terrible spirit, with neither hoofs, nor tail, nor horns; it is you who have endowed him with these attributes! But... he is not the question just now!"

JOHNNIE DAWES, *laughing hysterically*: "How do you know he is not the question now?"

LEBEDEV: "Another excellent idea, and worth considering!"

BERTRAM SCUDDER: "But, again, that is not the question. The question at this moment is whether we have not weakened *the springs of life* by the extension..."

AYN, *eagerly:* "Of railways?"

LEBEDEV: "Not railways, properly speaking, presumptuous youth, but the general tendency of which railways may be considered as the outward expression and symbol. We hurry and push and hustle, for the good of humanity! '*The world is becoming too noisy, too commercial!*' groans some solitary thinker. '*Undoubtedly it is, but the noise of wagons bearing bread to starving humanity is of more value than tranquillity of soul,*' replies another triumphantly, and passes on with an air of pride. As for me, I don't believe in these wagons bringing bread to humanity. For, founded on no moral principle, these may well, even in the act of carrying bread to humanity, coldly exclude a considerable portion of humanity from enjoying it; that has been seen more than once."

EDDIE WILLERS: "What, these wagons may coldly exclude?"

AYN, *shrugs:* "If civilization is to survive, it is the morality of altruism that men have to reject."

LEBEDEV, *not deigning to notice the interruption:* "That has been seen already. Malthus was a friend of humanity, but, with ill-founded moral principles, the friend of humanity is the devourer of humanity, without mentioning his pride; for, touch the vanity of one of these numberless philanthropists, and to avenge his self-esteem, he will be ready at once to set fire to the whole globe; and to tell the truth, we are all more or less like that. I, perhaps, might be the first to set a light to the fuel, and then run away. But, again, I must repeat, that is not the question."

SOMEONE: "What is it then, for goodness' sake?"

SOMEONE ELSE: "He is boring us!"

LEBEDEV: "The question is connected with the following anecdote of past times; for I am obliged to relate a story. In our times, and in our country, which I hope you love as much as I do, for as far as I am concerned, I am ready to shed the last drop of my blood..."

ALL: "Go on! Go on!"

LEBEDEV: "In our dear country, as indeed in the whole of Europe, a famine visits humanity about four times a century, as far as I can remember; once in every twenty-five years. I won't swear to this being the exact figure, but anyhow they have become comparatively rare."

BERTRAM SCUDDER, *sarcastically:* "Comparatively to what?"

LEBEDEV: "To the twelfth century, and those immediately preceding and following it. We are told by historians that widespread famines occurred in those days every two or three years, and such was the condition of things that men actually had recourse to cannibalism, in secret, of course. One of these cannibals, who had reached a good age, declared of his own free will that during the

Act III Scene II

course of his long and miserable life he had personally killed and eaten, in the most profound secrecy, sixty monks, not to mention several children; the number of the latter he thought was about six, an insignificant total when compared with the enormous mass of ecclesiastics consumed by him. As to adults, laymen that is to say, he had never touched them."

A general outcry.

Mr. Thompson: "That's impossible! I am often discussing subjects of this nature with him, gentlemen, but for the most part he talks nonsense enough to make one deaf: this story has no pretence of being true."

Lebedev: "Remember the siege of Kars! And you, gentlemen, I assure you my anecdote is the naked truth. I may remark that reality, although it is governed by invariable law, has at times a resemblance to falsehood. In fact, the truer a thing is the less true it sounds."

Someone, *scoffing in objection*: "But could anyone possibly eat sixty monks?"

Lebedev: "It is quite clear that he did not eat them all at once, but in a space of fifteen or twenty years: from that point of view the thing is comprehensible and natural..."

Bertram Scudder: "Natural?"

Lebedev, *with pedantic obstinacy*: "And natural."

Lebedev: "Besides, a Catholic monk is by nature excessively curious; it would be quite easy therefore to entice him into a wood, or some secret place, on false pretences, and there to deal with him as said. But I do not dispute in the least that the number of persons consumed appears to denote a spice of greediness."

> *Prince Myshkin has been listening in silence up to that moment without taking part in the conversation, but laughing heartily with the others from time to time. Evidently he is delighted to see that everybody was amused, that everybody is*

talking at once, and even that everybody is drinking

PRINCE MYSHKIN, *quietly*: "It is perhaps true, gentlemen."

PRINCE MYSHKIN, *seeming as if he were not intending to speak more, suddenly, in such a serious voice that everyone looks at him with interest*: "It is true that there were frequent famines at that time, gentlemen. I have often heard of them, though I do not know much history. But it seems to me that it must have been so.

When I was in Switzerland I used to look with astonishment at the many ruins of feudal castles perched on the top of steep and rocky heights, half a mile at least above sea-level, so that to reach them one had to climb many miles of stony tracks. A castle, as you know, is, a kind of mountain of stones — a dreadful, almost an impossible, labour! Doubtless the builders were all poor men, vassals, and had to pay heavy taxes, and to keep up the priesthood. How, then, could they provide for themselves, and when had they time to plough and sow their fields? The greater number must, literally, have died of starvation.

I have sometimes asked myself how it was that these communities were not utterly swept off the face of the earth, and how they could possibly survive. Lebedev is not mistaken, in my opinion, when he says that there were cannibals in those days, perhaps in considerable numbers; but I do not understand why he should have dragged in the monks, nor what he means by that."

BERTRAM SCUDDER: "It is undoubtedly because, in the twelfth century, monks were the only people one could eat; they were the fat, among many lean!"

LEBEDEV, *triumphantly*: "A brilliant idea, and most true! For he never even touched the laity. Sixty monks, and not a single layman!

It is a terrible idea, but it is historic, it is statistic; it is indeed one of those facts which enables an intelligent historian to reconstruct the physiognomy of a special epoch, for it brings out this further point with mathematical accuracy, that the clergy were in those days sixty times richer and more flourishing than the rest of humanity. And perhaps sixty times fatter also..."

MR. THOMPSON, *amid laughter:* "You are exaggerating, you are exaggerating, Lebedev!"

PRINCE MYSHKIN, *speaking so seriously that his tone contrasts quite comically with that of the others:* "I admit that it is an historic thought, but what is your conclusion?"

The others are very nearly laughing at him, too, but he does not notice it.

SOMEONE, *whispering in Prince Myshkin's ear:* "Don't you see he is a lunatic, Prince? Someone told me just now that he is a bit touched on the subject of lawyers, that he has a mania for making speeches and intends to pass the examinations. I am expecting a splendid burlesque now."

LEBEDEV, *in a voice like thunder:* "My conclusion is vast!"

LEBEDEV: "Let us examine first the psychological and legal position of the criminal. We see that in spite of the difficulty of finding other food, the accused, or, as we may say, my client, has often during his peculiar life exhibited signs of repentance, and of wishing to give up this clerical diet. Incontrovertible facts prove this assertion. He has eaten five or six children, a relatively insignificant number, no doubt, but remarkable enough from another point of view. It is manifest that, pricked by remorse — for my client is religious, in his way, and has a conscience, as I shall prove later — and desiring to extenuate his sin as far as possible, he has tried six times at least to substitute lay nourishment for clerical.

That this was merely an experiment we can hardly doubt: for if it had been only a question of gastronomic variety, six would have been too few; why only six? Why not thirty?

But if we regard it as an experiment, inspired by the fear of committing new sacrilege, then this number six becomes intelligible. Six attempts to calm his remorse, and the pricking of his conscience, would amply suffice, for these attempts could scarcely have been happy ones. In my humble opinion, a child is too small; I should say, not sufficient; which would result in four or five times more lay children than monks being required in a given time. The sin, lessened on the one hand, would therefore be increased on the other, in quantity, not in quality. Please understand, gentlemen, that in reasoning thus, I am taking the point of view which might have been taken by a criminal of the middle ages. As for myself, a man of our present times, I, of course, should reason differently;

I say so plainly, and therefore you need not jeer at me nor mock me, gentlemen." (*addressing Mr. Thompson*) "As for you, Mr President, it is still more unbecoming on your part." (*turning back to the others*) "In the second place, and giving my own personal opinion, a child's flesh is not a satisfying diet; it is too insipid, too sweet; and the criminal, in making these experiments, could have satisfied neither his conscience nor his appetite. I am about to conclude, gentlemen;

And my conclusion contains a reply to one of the most important questions of that day and of our own! This criminal ended at last by denouncing himself to the clergy, and giving himself up to justice. We cannot but ask, remembering the penal system of that day, and the tortures that awaited him — the wheel, the stake, the fire! — We cannot but ask, I repeat, what induced him to accuse himself of this crime? Why did he not simply stop short at the number sixty, and keep his secret until his last breath? Why could he not simply leave the monks alone, and go into the desert to repent? Or why not become a monk himself? That is where the puzzle comes in! There must have been something stronger than the stake or the fire, or even than the habits of twenty years! There must have been an idea more powerful than all the calamities and sorrows of this world, famine or torture, leprosy or plague — an idea which entered into the heart, directed and enlarged the springs of life, and made even that hell supportable to humanity!

Show me a force, a power like that, in this our century of vices and railways! I might say, perhaps, in our century of steamboats and railways, but I repeat in our century of vices and railways, because I am drunk but truthful! Show me a single idea which unites men nowadays with half the strength that it had in those centuries, and dare to maintain that the *springs of life* have not been polluted and weakened beneath this *star*, beneath this network in which men are entangled! Don't talk to me about your prosperity, your riches, the rarity of famine, the rapidity of the means of transport! There is more of riches, but less of force. The idea uniting heart and soul to heart and soul exists no more!"

AYN, JOHN GALT, FRANCISCO D'ANCONIA AND RAGNAR DANNESKJÖLD *step forward and recite in solemn, triumphant unity:*

"I swear by my life and my love of it that I will never live for the sake of another man, nor ask another man to live for mine!"

An angelic chorus answers the Galtian Oath...

Chorus: "John Henry" (Key of C)

This is the hammer that killed John Henry
This is the hammer that killed John Henry,
This is the hammer that killed John Henry,
But it won't kill me, Lord, but it won't kill me.

Transition to Eddie Willers' living room...

Scene III — John Henry

Time: Just before dawn...

Place: Eddie Willers' apartment.

Cast: Eddie Willers

> *Eddie, sprawled on the sofa, wakes from his nightmare. On the radio, he hears...*
>> *This is the hammer that killed John Henry*
>> *This is the hammer that killed John Henry,*
>> *This is the hammer that killed John Henry,*
>> *But it won't kill me, Lord, but it won't kill me.*
>
> *A ringing phone. Eddie answers.*

Eddie Willers: "Hello..."

> *pauses to listen*

Eddie Willers: "What?"

> *pauses to listen*

Eddie Willers: "A wreck?" *(listens)* "On the Kansas-Southern?"

> *pauses to listen*

Eddie Willers: "That bad?"

> *pauses to listen*

Eddie Willers: "Yes, yes, I'll be right in..."

Musical Scores

Songs adapted from "American Negro Songs"
Crown Publishers, Inc, New York in 1940

"I ask for nothing, I can get by,
but I know so many less lucky than I..."

Music Scores

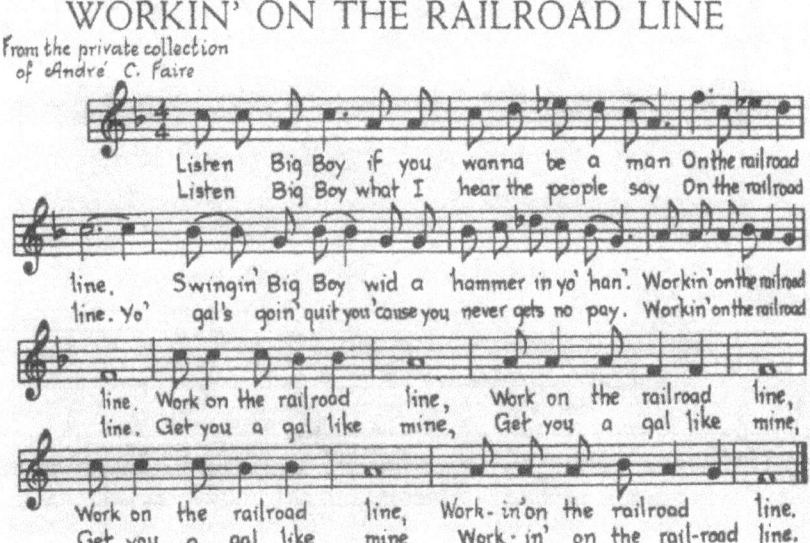

Illustrations

Madras famine of 1877, (Page 5), uncounted thousands starved while cargos of grain were loaded for export before their eyes.

"Ganymede" (Page 23) F. Kirchback, Artist
Inspired by Homer's *Illiad*
Character Sketches of Romance, Fiction and Drama
Selmar Hess Press, 1892,

"Mephistopheles and Faust" (Page 31) A. Jacomin, Artist
Inspired by Goethe's *Faust*
Ibid.

"Colonel Newcome" (Page 73) Frederick Bernard, Artist
Inspired by Thackeray's *The Newcomes*
Ibid.

"Sir Amyas Leigh" (Page 89) C.J. Staniland, Artist
Inspired by Charles Kingsley's *Westward Ho!*
Ibid.

"Esmerelda" (Page 111) G. Bryon, Artist
Inspired by Victor Hugo's *Notre Dame de Paris*
Ibid.

www.speedofdark.com

www.ingramcontent.com/pod-product-compliance
Lightning Source LLC
LaVergne TN
LVHW041630070426
835507LV00008B/545